'Tests . . . can still be but the beginning, never the end, of the examination of a child. To take a young mind as it is, and delicately one by one to sound its notes and stops, to detect the smaller discords and appreciate the subtler harmonies, is more of an art than a science. The scientist may standardise the method; to apply that method and to appraise the results, demands the tact, the experience, the imaginative insight of the teacher born and trained.'

Sir C. Burt: *Mental and Scholastic Tests*.

EDUCATION TODAY
For a full list of titles in this series, see back cover

A Teacher's Guide to Tests and Testing

Third edition

STEPHEN JACKSON, M.ED.
Head of the Department
for Special and Remedial Education
Jordanhill College of Education
Glasgow

LONGMAN

17702

LONGMAN GROUP LIMITED
London
*Associated companies, branches and representatives
throughout the world*

© Longman Group Ltd 1968, 1971, 1974

First published 1968
Second edition 1971
Third edition 1974
Second impression 1975
Third impression 1977

ISBN 0 582 18140 2

*Printed in Hong Kong by
Sheck Wah Tong Printing Press*

Contents

PREFACE TO THIRD EDITION   vii

GLOSSARY OF TERMS   viii

INTRODUCTION   x

PART ONE. THE NATURE OF TESTS AND INTER-
PRETATION OF RESULTS

1   Test Sources   3

2   Choosing a Test   9

3   Using and Misusing Tests   17

4   Testing Mental Ability   23

5   Current Trends in Intelligence Testing   40

PART TWO. DETAILS OF TESTS

6   Mental Tests for the Pre-School Child   56

7   Mental Ability Tests which Include Items for Infants   59

8   Mental Ability Tests for Seven-Year-Olds   71

9   Non-Reading Mental Ability Tests for Ages between 6
and 14 years   74

    Non-Reading Mental Ability Tests for Ages between 10
and 16 years   76

10   Verbal Mental Ability Tests for Ages between 6 and
13 years   78

    Verbal Mental Ability Tests for Ages between 10 and
13 years   80

    Verbal Mental Ability Tests for Ages between 10 and
16 years   81

    Verbal Mental Ability Tests for Higher Levels of
Reasoning   83

11   Readiness for Reading   85

12	Testing Reading	96
	Individual Tests of Reading	101
	Group Tests of Reading	105
	Diagnostic Tests Related to Reading	110
13	Tests of Number Readiness	115
14	Tests of Arithmetic and Mathematics	122
	Diagnostic Tests of Arithmetic	126
15	Tests of English	129
16	Test Batteries	134
17	Tests of Social Adaptation, Aptitude, Interest and Personality	137
	APPENDIX 1 Tips for Testers	149
	APPENDIX 2	150
	Rank and Product-Moment Correlation	150
	Mean and Standard Deviation	152
	Table for Relating Percentile Scores to Standard Scores	153
	FURTHER READING	154
	LIST OF ADDRESSES OF TEST PUBLISHERS	155
	INDEX OF TEST TITLES	157
	GENERAL INDEX	160

Preface to Second Edition

Since this book was first published a number of developments have made a new edition necessary. New tests of reading, general ability, and language development have appeared. Decimalisation, metrication and new methods of teaching mathematics have caused the demise of old and the creation of new mathematics tests. The reorganisation of schools has blurred the meaning of the words junior, primary and secondary, causing the National Foundation for Educational Research to retitle many of their tests. Several tests described in the first edition as unsuited to present needs have been withdrawn or discontinued.

In response to readers' suggestions, several minor amendments have been made; the Glossary and Further Reading List have been extended, and the last two chapters of the first edition have been extended and organised into a single chapter.

With the passing of time many tests become invalid and I am most grateful to those authors and publishers who have sent me their latest productions, and thus made it possible to provide information on tests that meet the needs of today.

Preface to Third Edition

Changes in the third edition are largely confined to the section on test details, due to tests such as Schonell's Mechanical Arithmetic, Manchester Reading Comprehension Test, Lambert's Seven Plus Spelling Test, going out of print; and the publishing of important new tests such as the Edinburgh Reading Tests, Thackray's Reading Readiness Profiles, and Young's Oral Verbal Intelligence Test. The first section of the book remains relatively unchanged.

Glossary of Terms

APTITUDE. Capacity to learn. Aptitude tests are usually tests for special aptitude, e.g. for music.

ATTAINMENT AGE. Level of attainment in a subject expressed in terms of the average age at which that level is reached.

ATTAINMENT QUOTIENT (A.Q.). The ratio of attainment-age to what is expected. But expectation may be based on life-age or mental-age. Thus a reading quotient of a 10-year-old with a reading-age of 8 and a mental-age of 9 could be either 80 or 90.

ATTAINMENT TEST. A test for measuring achievement in a particular skill, e.g. reading or arithmetic.

BATTERY. A test-battery is a group of tests standardised on the same population and dealing with related subjects.

COGNITION. A process by which the mind becomes aware of what is perceived or conceived; an act of knowing in contrast with an act of willing or feeling.

CORRELATION. The relationship between two variables indicating that a change in one is accompanied by a change in the other.

CORRELATION COEFFICIENT. A number between -1.0 and $+1.0$ showing the amount of correspondence between two variables.

DIAGNOSTIC TEST. A test for detecting the detailed nature of a disability rather than the level of attainment.

EXTRAPOLATE. To continue a curve on a graph by inference from the existing curve and without supporting data.

GROUP TEST. A test that can be given to several people at the same time by one tester.

MEAN. Commonly called the average, the sum of a set of scores divided by the number of scores.

MEDIAN. The middle score. In any set of scores, half of the scores are higher and half are lower than the median.

viii

MODE. The score which occurs most often in a set of scores.

MENTAL-ABILITY TEST. A term used in this book in preference to the more abused term 'intelligence test', and indicating a test for measuring some aspect or aspects of mental development.

NORMS. Sets of scores which are representative for certain types or groups, e.g. persons of a certain age, and with which any individual score can be compared and thus given meaning.

OBJECTIVE TEST. A test given and scored according to a set procedure that is independent of the tester's subjective judgement.

OMNIBUS TEST. A test which measures a variety of abilities and in which the items are presented in a mixed sequence rather than grouped according to type.

PARALLEL TEST. One that may be used as an alternative to the original and yields very similar scores.

PERFORMANCE TEST. A test that involves physical action rather than words, and measures ability to deal with objects rather than symbols.

PROJECTION TEST. A test in which the subject is encouraged to respond freely to stimuli such as ink-blots, ambiguous drawings, and thus project his feelings and ideas.

RAW SCORES. The scores actually made on a test before being corrected or converted to, for example, age levels or standard scores.

STANDARD DEVIATION. A measure of the extent to which a set of scores are scattered above and below the mean score. It is arrived at by finding the amount by which each score deviates from the mean, squaring each deviation, averaging these squares, then finding the square root of that average.

STANDARD ERROR. The amount by which an actual test-score differs from a hypothetical 'true score'.

STANDARD SCORES. These are obtained by converting raw scores to a standard scale. In most British tests a standard score of 100 is used to represent the middle raw score of the group for which the test is intended, and the range is usually from about 70 to 140.

STANDARDISED TEST. A test whose scoring, norms and administration have been established as a result of the test being tried out on large numbers of subjects.

TRUE SCORE. A person's test-score is affected by variables that cannot be perfectly controlled. A true score is a hypothetical score, free of such influences.

Introduction

The comment that followed John T. all through his primary school years was: 'When you talk to him he seems quite bright; and yet he just cannot learn to read.' When he was twelve a reading specialist asked his teacher what was being done to help him and was told: 'I just keep pegging away hoping the penny will drop.'

Whether the penny would ever have dropped is questionable. What is certain is that the reading specialist, by the use of a test of non-verbal ability and diagnostic reading tests, quickly identified John's specific difficulties, and was able to plan remedial lessons that soon led to literacy.

Jane P. was a child whose response to lessons was extremely erratic. She was frequently reported to look bewildered when asked the simplest of questions. She was ten and a half when an observant teacher thought to give her a simple hearing test and discovered that she had a hearing loss in both ears, the loss being particularly severe in one ear. After a hearing-aid had been fitted her general progress and emotional stability noticeably improved.

These are but two examples of the way in which a knowledge of simple tests for use in school can help the child realise his full potential. Similar incidents occur daily. It is perhaps not tests of this nature that people have in mind when they think of school tests. In recent years so much publicity has surrounded the eleven plus examination that little thought has been given to the many other kinds of tests that can contribute to the child's welfare, and which are described in this book.

It must also be said that even though selection for secondary schools is disappearing, streaming is under fire, and faith in the intelligence test has been rudely, albeit unjustly, shaken, there is still a need for objective tests of ability and attainment. A closer look at some of these changes shows that they reflect not a loss of faith in objective tests but a rethinking of their purpose.

When it appeared that the Government intended to introduce comprehensive education on a wide scale, the National Foundation for Educational Research canvassed local education authorities as to their future need of standardised tests, and were assured[1] that such tests would be required for a long time to come. There are several reasons for this. Where the eleven plus has been dropped the teachers themselves may be responsible for any classification requested from the receiving secondary schools, and may, therefore, take an increased interest in techniques that can help them to provide assessments.

Comprehensive schools are under pressure from their critics to justify the abolition of grammar schools and show that the change has not meant a levelling down, that the claimed ease of transfer between streams is a reality, and that the late developer really is detected and nurtured. In the achievement of these goals, objective tests can play a vital part.

Where non-streaming has been adopted this can be seen, not as a determination to treat all children alike, but as a concern for the individual child. The teacher faced with a class of widely varying abilities will be better equipped to meet this challenge if she has the kind of detailed appraisal of each child which will enable her to plan work or experiences at levels appropriate to the pupil's abilities.

The discrediting of the 'intelligence' test has been due less to the inefficiency of the tests than to the misguided expectations of what such tests could do. We know now that a single I.Q. figure is merely a rough guide, and that a wide variety of tests is necessary in order to make a realistic assessment of a child's resources.

One of the most striking features in education today is a sharper awareness of individual differences, shown in the growing provision of special courses, special schools, remedial centres, diagnostic units, and the encouragement of 'discovery methods'. This awareness has been due in no small measure to improved techniques in measuring the social, intellectual, and emotional qualities of children.

For a long time British educators have restricted their use of

[1] N.F.E.R. Annual Report, 1965/6.

objective tests of attainment to a few subjects, but very recently there has appeared a readiness to consider their wider application, for example trial runs[1] for the C.S.E. examination convinced the Schools Council that the objective-type test merited further investigation as a suitable method for testing C.S.E. candidates, and Leeds University has used objective tests for first-year students of psychology and sociology.

It is often said that research in education is done too often by people who have little day-to-day contact with children and whose choice of research topic rarely serves a practical end. When teachers themselves receive better briefing on the use and value of tests we might well see an increase in small but valuable studies carried out by those who know which problems are most urgent and who are most likely to profit from the results.

Schools are now being bombarded with advertising matter tempting them to buy this or that teaching machine, reading scheme or number apparatus: how successful these aids may be remains a matter of opinion and prejudice until their effect has been carefully checked by the use of reliable attainment tests.

From the teachers' point of view, the main purposes of educational tests are:

1. TO MEASURE LEARNING ABILITY. There is only one kind of effective teaching and that is the kind that results in effective learning. To determine the level and the pace at which teaching is likely to be successful it is necessary to have (a) an estimate of the pupil's present knowledge of the subject and (b) an estimate of the pupil's ability to learn. This information can most quickly be obtained by the use of tests of attainment and mental ability.

2. TO COMPARE PUPILS. Where pupils are to be allotted to teaching groups or classes, tests are needed which will discriminate finely. Here teacher-made tests may be adequate, but if a comparison of school or class with a national standard is needed then it will be essential to use a test that has been standardised on a large population.

[1] *Examinations Bulletin* No. 14, H.M.S.O., 1966.

3. MEASURE PROGRESS. Teachers measure individual progress in their own ways, week by week, using their own tests and observations. But where objectivity and comparison with normal progress is needed, standardised tests may be preferable.

4. TO DIAGNOSE DIFFICULTIES. If tests of progress have shown that a child is not doing as well as may be reasonably expected, then diagnostic tests may be used to identify particular weaknesses: in arithmetic this may concern a specific process or number bond; in reading, a tendency to sound the first letter and guess the rest; in motivation, a persistent fear of failure.

5. TO COMPARE SCHOOLS. Administrators may wish to compare schools within their area. While internal standards can be used to compare pupils within a school, the comparison of one school with another requires the use of an external standard. This need not be a nationally standardised test. It could be one standardised on a city or a county: in the case of Manchester, for example, schools may be compared with each other, by using the Manchester Reading Comprehension Test, and the Manchester General Ability Test.

6. IN RESEARCH. Not only research by research students but investigations by teachers in their schools, perhaps to evaluate the use of apparatus or a teaching method, call for initial and final tests of an objective kind.

In the last analysis, all these purposes can be summed up in one: to enable the teacher to teach more effectively, and therefore the child to learn more efficiently.

While the making of objective tests is an expert's job the responsibility of using and interpreting results often rests with the teacher. Not all teachers want to be test experts, but head teachers should be aware of the need to ensure that suitable tests are chosen and that they are given correctly.

The following pages are in two main sections. The first is largely concerned with the nature and use of tests and the interpretation of results. The second includes details of over 150 tests of mental ability, arithmetic, reading, English, spelling, aptitudes, personality and social adjustment. It is hoped that the first section will help both students and teachers to understand the merits and the limitations of tests and thus lead them to use tests wisely; the second section, by its arrangement and comment, will make possible the speedy selection of specific tests to suit particular purposes.

Part One

The Nature of Tests and Interpretation of Results

I

Test Sources

Teachers can obtain tests from two main sources, (*a*) The National Foundation for Educational Research and (*b*) commercial publishers, of whom the most prolific are the University of London Press, Harrap and Company, Oliver and Boyd, and Gibson and Son. With the exception of a few 'closed'[1] and restricted tests to be referred to later, these tests can be bought by any school direct from the publisher. They are unlikely to be found in bookshops unless they are part of a book, as for example, Burt's *Mental and Scholastic Tests*.

It must be said that the test details in publishers' catalogues are often not reliable enough to justify a confident purchase. Publishers commit sins of omission. For example, one offers a mental ability test to British teachers without mentioning that it was made for American children forty years ago and has been superseded by an improved test by the same author. It is, therefore, advisable to see a test before placing a sizeable order. Publishers[2] will send a specimen set if asked, and this should include a copy of each item necessary for giving the test, e.g. a marking key, instruction manual, answer paper or pupil's booklet. Visual inspection is not enough; only by trying out the test can snags in administration, marking and scoring be discovered.

It would be unduly optimistic to expect commercial publishers to protect their customers by withdrawing out-of-date tests and to

[1] For example, tests to be used for public examinations and available only to those responsible for administering them.
[2] Publishers' addresses will be found in the Appendix.

demand from their authors standards of presentation and construction that would satisfy the British Psychological Society. Fortunately there are two other sources whose aim is not to make a profit but to serve the best interests of the schools. These are the National Foundation for Educational Research (N.F.E.R.) and Moray House. Since both play a large part in British education, and their function is not always understood, a brief outline of their work is given here.

The N.F.E.R.

The N.F.E.R. was founded in 1946 and is 'a partnership of all concerned with public education in England and Wales'. It is financed by contributions from local education authorities, universities, colleges of advanced technology, national associations of teachers, H.M. Forces, and a grant-in-aid from the Department of Education and Science. The Foundation undertakes research on a contractual basis for Government departments, and may receive money from any individual or institution to support its general work or initiate research. Its work has developed in response to the expressed needs of the schools and colleges, and its functions now include:

1. RESEARCH. The Foundation has organised many projects to investigate current educational problems on a national scale, e.g. Streaming in the Primary School, Comprehensive Education, French in Primary Schools. Many important publications have resulted from research sponsored by the N.F.E.R., e.g. *Progress in Reading* (1966) by Joyce Morris.

2. INFORMATION SERVICE. Enquiries are invited from individuals or institutions on questions concerning testing or research. Publications include a thrice-yearly journal, *Educational Research* informing teachers of the latest findings in educational research and written in a readable non-academic style; 'technical education abstracts', to keep teachers in technical education abreast of recent developments; and 'occasional publications' which are intended to make available special matter which would not normally be published in book form, e.g. *Recent Studies in Britain Based on the Work of Jean Piaget* (1961) by E. Lunzer.

3. TEST CONSTRUCTION. The N.F.E.R. is now one of the major test-producing agencies of the English speaking world. For many years it has supplied Directors of Education with 'closed' tests which are available to no one else. It also produces open tests for the use of class teachers and for district surveys; these cover reading, English, arithmetic, mathematics. New tests are added from time to time and old tests withdrawn or restandardised. A full list of these with descriptions, prices and advice on their use will be found in the N.F.E.R. catalogue called *Tests for Guidance and Assessment*, obtainable from Ginn and Co, 18 Bedford Row, London, W.C.1.

4. TEST AGENCY. Since many of the tests found valuable by teachers and research workers originate in other countries, the N.F.E.R. acts as an agency to facilitate distribution, holding stocks and supplying tests as required. These tests, listed in the *Test Agency Catalogue*, cover a wide variety of topics, e.g. personality, mechanical aptitude, social maturity, anxiety, interest, colour discrimination, but not all of them are available to the class teacher. The N.F.E.R. takes the view that many of these are delicate psychological instruments to be used with great care, and is careful to supply them only to suitably qualified persons.

Who Qualifies as a Tester?

The N.F.E.R. Test Agency grades its tests A, P, Q, R, K, L. *Level A* tests require a minimum amount of technical knowledge and can be obtained by any school. *Level P* tests can only be used by those qualified by successful attendance at a course of training in test administration and interpretation which is acceptable to the Test Agency, or by a person who can produce evidence of experience in the use of tests (under the guidance of someone qualified by training) which the Test Agency may recognise as equivalent. *Level Q* tests can be used only by a qualified psychologist; this qualification entails at least a degree in psychology or the level of Associate Member of the British Psychological Society.

Tests labelled R, K and L are unlikely to be used by teachers; the required qualifications are printed in the Test Agency Catalogue, 1970.

Moray House

For many years British teachers have used, marked, and discussed Moray House tests, especially in connection with eleven plus tests, but few have known what kind of establishment produced these tests. Sir Godfrey Thomson was one of the early pioneers in test construction and his Moray House Tests set standards which have been followed by many others both at home and abroad. The tests get their name from the fact that the University department in which Thomson worked was housed in the same building as the Moray House College of Education. Although tests are no longer produced in Moray House the name is retained as a kind of trade mark. Moray House Tests are actually produced by the Godfrey Thomson Unit for Educational Research. Unlike the N.F.E.R. this unit receives no financial support from local or national government. It is an integral part of Edinburgh University and is financed almost entirely from profits on the sale of tests. Its usual customers are Directors of Education to whom it supplies 'closed' tests. Individuals may in special circumstances obtain such tests but only with the permission of the local Director of Education. At the time of writing teachers cannot obtain tests directly from the unit but may buy through the University of London Press certain of the unit's tests which were originally closed but have now been made available for general use, e.g. Picture Test 1, which is a mental-ability test for seven-year-olds. The decreasing demand for eleven plus tests has made it possible for the unit to embark on producing tests which are in line with the changes now taking place in the teaching of school subjects, especially in mathematics and English.

How a standardised test is made

When a teacher wants to check her pupils' progress it is usually sufficient for her to make her own test, based upon the class syllabus. But if a comparison with a much bigger, perhaps a national, population is wanted then a widely standardised test constructed by a professional test-maker will be needed. This does not mean that standardised tests are made without any reference to the teacher in the classroom. Tests arise from practical needs, which may range

6

from the need to identify reading-readiness to the selection of university entrants, and teachers are almost invariably called in to help the test specialist by (a) ensuring that the content of the test is suited to the abilities of the pupils and to the objectives of the schools and (b) helping to administer the try-out tests that are necessary before the final version is printed.

The construction of a standardised test is a long and complex procedure but its main features may be outlined as follows. Among the earliest decisions to be made are those concerning the duration of the test and the number of items. It must be long enough to measure what it is intended to measure, short enough to be given conveniently within the framework of the school timetable, and not too tiring for the type of child in mind. Here, experience in test-making can save a great deal of wasted effort.

After content and length have been decided, the next step is the writing of the items. Many more are needed than will be included in the final version, for an item must be proved to be effective before it can be finally adopted. From this collection preliminary tests are assembled, each containing the required number of items, and these are tried out on a group of children similar in age, ability and background to those for whom the final version is intended.

The results of the try-out tests are carefully examined to see (a) how well the test as a whole discriminates among the children— this will show whether the test is so easy or so hard that it requires drastic modification and (b) how well each item contributes to the total effectiveness of the test. In examining (b) a process is carried out called item analysis. Each item is given a difficulty-rating by finding out the percentage of children getting it right. This makes it possible to manipulate the items in such a way as to increase or decrease difficulty in any section of the test. It is also necessary to find out how far success or failure on a particular item is associated with a high or low total score. To do this the test papers are arranged in order of merit (according to total scores) then the top quarter and the bottom quarter are compared, item by item. If, say, 90 per cent of the children in the top quarter but only 5 per cent in the bottom quarter get an item right, then that item is clearly discriminating between the bright and the less bright. But if an item is correctly answered by 90 per cent in the top quarter and by 80 per cent in the

7

bottom quarter then that item would be a poor discriminator and might be discarded. If an item is answered correctly by more of the bottom quarter than the top quarter, this would warrant a careful search to see what had led the brighter children along the wrong track.

Wrong answers would also be studied to see whether too many children had given the same wrong answers: if this were the case, and especially if these wrong answers had been given by the brighter pupils, these items would be examined for ambiguity, and rewritten or discarded. New items introduced would have to be checked not only for their discriminatory power and their difficulty-rating but for their actual content in terms of subject matter.

After these revisions had been made, the tests would be given to a new group of suitable children, and lead to further item analysis and modification. Eventually an array of suitable items would be formed into the final version. The last step would be standardisation. This would be done by giving the test to a large number of children, often several thousand, carefully chosen for whatever attributes were thought necessary, e.g. age, sex, social and geographical background, and on the basis of these test-scores a norms table[1] would be constructed. This table, usually supplied with each test manual, gives the scores achieved by children representatives of a certain age, sex and background; in other words a standard of normal achievement against which the teacher can compare the scores of her own pupils.

While the actual process of constructing a test is much more complicated than has been outlined here, these are the basic stages; details would vary according to the nature and purpose of the test.[2]

[1] See page 36 for an example.
[2] For a fuller account see *Objective Testing* by Macintosh and Morrison, U.L.P., 1969.

2

Choosing a Test

Individual or group?

There are several reasons why certain tests have to be given individually: the child may be required to speak his answers, the tester may need to watch and record how the child behaves or manipulates apparatus, it may be necessary to follow up a child's particular responses by supplementary questions or, in the case of very young children, their very immaturity may call for the intimacy and security of a one-to-one relationship.

Where a precise and detailed assessment is required, e.g. for Child Guidance purposes, or when transfer to a special school is considered, then an individual test will be called for. Individual tests are often more searching than group tests, allowing as they do a close observance of the child and in some cases a certain amount of flexibility in the tester's approach. As one would expect, skill in the use of certain individual tests, such as the Stanford-Binet Intelligence Scale, requires a considerable amount of training and experience.

When group tests are given, each child marks his or her responses on an answer paper by underlining, writing, ringing, etc. The tests are often carefully timed, the whole group starting and finishing at the supervisor's word. Very little training is needed for the giving of group tests and they are comparatively easy to mark and score. Where large numbers have to be tested, group tests are economical in time and labour. They can, of course, be given individually if there is only one child to be tested and the issue is not very serious, but on the whole they are used for surveys of classes, schools, and larger populations.

How old is it?

Most books on testing suggest that a test can best be judged by
finding the answer to two questions: Is it reliable? Is it valid?
These questions are crucial and will be dealt with below, but there
are others which are also important and whose answers moreover do
not involve even the simplest of statistics.

All tests date. They date in three main ways. Firstly, as the
standards of general education throughout the country change, so
too must the norm, the average level of achievement, upon which
the scoring of a test is based at the time it is made. For example,
the standard of prose reading in English schools rose significantly[1]
between 1948 and 1956, nine months in the case of older juniors and
five months in the case of the secondary modern pupils. *This means
that the standards given as normal in any prose-reading test made earlier than
1948 are now quite invalid. This would include many of the tests widely used
and quoted today. e.g. most of the tests by Burt, Schonell, Vernon and Watts.*

Secondly, not only do standards change but so also does the
content of what is taught in schools. This is inevitable if progress
continues to be made. But this means that tests must be continually
revised and adapted to the needs of the schools. If children are
taught mathematics by the discovery method then an appropriate
mathematics test should measure their ability to make mathematical
discoveries, not merely the ability to compute or solve formal
problems.

Thirdly, it should be remembered that most intelligence tests,
excepting those that are culture-free, i.e. free from any symbol
reflecting current culture, are based on the assumption that the
pupil has a store of knowledge that has been acquired with a
minimum of intelligence by simple living in the contemporary
world. For example, picture-intelligence tests often require the child
to classify pictures of objects; but he can scarcely do this if he does
not even recognise them. The social scene changes, and in areas of
city redevelopment sometimes with bewildering rapidity. Fresh
styles appear in buildings, furniture, toys, transport, dress, and some
come to stay. With these social changes, and often resulting from
them, comes changes in children's vocabulary; words familiar to one

[1] *Standards of Reading—1948-56*, H.M.S.O.

generation are unfamiliar to the next. Clearly an intelligence test which assumes that the modern child is familiar with the social scene and vocabulary of the 1930s will not give valid results. Yet certain tests bought by the undiscriminating today contain anachronisms such as pictures of tram-cars, airships, steam engines, gas lamps, and words such as Condy's fluid, senna tea, carbolic powder, parlour maid. Any test which reflects the current social scene is in danger of becoming out-of-date within twenty years.

One of the few test-makers to warn against the dangers of using his own tests in places and at times for which they were never intended was, not surprisingly, Sir Cyril Burt. In introducing his own volume of tests he wrote: 'The chief purpose of the work is not to present the teacher with an automatic set of measuring scales suited to all localities and occasions, but to show by actual illustration how he can construct and standardise more appropriate versions for himself.'

Unfortunately Burt's advice has been too rarely taken. His exposition has been largely ignored, but his tests have been seized upon and used in situations which Burt himself would have said were unsuitable.

Is the test suited to the child?

In choosing a test one should ensure that it suits the child's *age*, *ability* and *background*. The stipulation about age is more necessary now that it used to be, for the modern tendency is to make tests for a narrow age range, often for only one year of age. For a quick coarse grading, short tests covering a wide age range may be useful, but they fail to give good discrimination at any particular level. A test containing fifty graded items designed only for seven-year-olds would give fifty possible grades; but a fifty-item test intended for children between seven and fourteen years would provide only about seven grades for each year of age. Many tests covering a wide age range are often unreliable at the extremes, and it is always safer to use them for the middle of the stated range.

Does the test suit the child's *ability*? This has a special relevance to intelligence or mathematics tests that require reading ability. Obviously it is no good giving a test of verbal reasoning or problem arithmetic to a child who cannot read. Yet this is often done, not because teachers do not appreciate the point just made, but because test manuals rarely warn that a certain level of reading is necessary. Where it is suspected that reading disability may interfere with assessing a child's reasoning power, it may be possible to find a test which covers similar thought-processes but couched in a non-reading medium, e.g. one given orally or in pictures.

Suiting the test to the child's ability also means making sure that the child's level is likely to be within the range of ability covered by the test. If a class to be tested includes many dull children, i.e. with I.Q.s below 85, one would avoid a test whose range covers only average and above average ability.

A glance at the table of normal scores in the test manual might reveal that the lowest I.Q. scorable for this age of child was 90. Many of the old grammar school selection tests gave fine grading among the brighter children, but children with I.Q.s under 90 found little that they could do on such tests.

To satisfy the third requirement, suiting the test to the child's *experience*, it is necessary to know where and on whom the test has been standardised. Social conditions and school standards differ not only from one generation to another but from one place to another at the same instant. A test standardised in Glasgow may be unsuitable for Cockneys and one standardised on British children may be unsuitable for newly-arrived immigrants. The whole purpose of using a standardised test is to compare a child's performance with that of other children *who have had very similar opportunities for learning*.

What exactly does the test test?

To order a test of reading or arithmetic or mental ability and in doing so believe that the test will measure the quintessence of reading or arithmetic or mental ability is an act of misguided trust. The user needs to decide exactly which mental process or particular skill he wishes to measure. Is the arithmetic test intended to measure computation, problem-solving ability, basic number concepts, or a combination of these? Is the reading test to consist of graded words, sentences or stories? Is it to be oral or silent? Is the mental test to be verbal or non-verbal, group or individual, practical or pencil-and-paper? Only a thorough scrutiny of the test will show what it measures and whether it will serve the particular purpose the user has in mind. The information given in the latter part of this book should help readers to make a wise selection.

Marking the test

If a large number of children are to be tested then the time and labour of marking needs to be considered. Some tests have the most ingenious marking systems, e.g. the Otis Quick Scoring Mental Ability Test, whose single cut-out stencil can be used, by turning it upside down and using both sides, to mark eight different pages of the test booklet. Others seem to create the maximum of difficulty and therefore the greatest chance of making mistakes in marking. If a quick, simple marking device or method is not included in the test manual then it may be worth while making one. A glance at methods already in use, transparent stencils, cut-out stencils, separate answer sheets, a marked test booklet, the technique of marking the first page of all the tests, then all the second pages and so on, may suggest the most appropriate one for the occasion. Whichever method is used, it is always a safe precaution to have the marking done again by a different person, perhaps using a different coloured pencil.

Conversion tables (see page 36 for an example)

Most norms tables are also conversion tables, for they usually show how raw scores, i.e. the actual marks earned on the test, can be converted to another type of score which makes possible the straight comparison of scores from different tests. But one needs to be sure that the type of converted score used on a test will be understood by those likely to be concerned in its use. Some prefer to express a score as an 'age', others prefer quotients, others can talk comfortably about quotients as applied to intelligence tests but prefer 'ages' when discussing reading ability, and still others would rather turn scores into simple percentiles. The relationships between these various kinds of converted scores are illustrated in the following pages. All that is being said here is that it is necessary to see that the tests chosen have conversion tables that are comprehensible to the users.

Reliability

When using a test frequently one needs to feel confident that it gives consistent results and is not likely to be construed in many different ways by different people. Can it stand up to use by different testers and their styles of presentation? Will it give similar result if given to the same children after a short interval of time? This type of reliability, sometimes referred to as stability, is measured by giving the test to a group of subjects, then after a short period giving it them again, then comparing the two sets of results. This is the test-retest method. If the order of merit is exactly the same at the second testing as at the first then the reliability is perfect and would be expressed by the figure 1. A simple example of how to work out a rank-order correlation is given in the Appendix. The reliability correlation figure for most published tests is usually between ·85 and ·99. A correlation figure derived from a retest-test of this kind should be above ·8 before the test can be considered reasonably reliable. If a test manual contains no evidence of the test's reliability, and as will be seen in Part Two of this book there are many such, it is possible that the actual reliability is low.

Another aspect of a test's reliability, usually referred to as internal consistency, is concerned with showing how far each item contributes to the value of the whole test. Does the test rely for its effectiveness on just a few items and are the others merely passengers? One way of checking this is by the split-half method. This consists of splitting the test, making one half all the odd items and the other half the even items, giving each half test on its own, and then comparing the scores. If all the items are contributing to a reasonable extent the results of the two separate tests should show high agreement. As in the test-retest method, the agreement is expressed as a decimal fraction, scores above ·8 being within an acceptable margin.

Validity

The validity of a university entrance examination, of an officer selection procedure, of choosing young girls for ballet-training, depends upon whether experience proves that the right choice has been made. If a test can be shown to measure what it purports to measure then, in test phraseology, the test is valid. There are two main kinds of validity; predictive and concurrent. Predictive validity is concerned with how well the test predicts the future performance of the subjects taking the test. Obviously it may be necessary to wait many years before evidence of this kind can be obtained. In some cases a very difficult question to answer is: at what point should we check on validity? In the case of the university entrance examination, should we accept degree examination results, or career achievement? Statements about predictive validity have to be hedged about with qualifying conditions concerning the period of time that should occur between test and retest.

It is much easier to measure concurrent validity. This means comparing the subject's performance on the test with their performance on some other test or work, which is accepted as testing much the same kind of thing as the first. Thus, it may be claimed that children do almost as well on a new short reading test, as they do on a lengthy long-established one. The scores made by the same group of children on the two tests may be correlated (just as in the test-retest technique) and the result quoted as a decimal figure.

Extracts from a fairly recent test manual are given below. The test referred to is the Non-Readers Intelligence Test by D. Young, and the following is a much abbreviated version of Young's validity and reliability data.

RELIABILITY (a) Stability. A retest of the same sample of 100 children after four weeks led to a Stability Coefficient of ·95. Another year group of 89 children of an average age of 7·6 was retested after ten months and a coefficient of ·88 calculated.

RELIABILITY (b) Internal consistency. There were two investigations using split-halves methods. One used the results of a year group of 100 children of average age of 8·0, the other a cross-section of the standardisation sample, 110 children aged 8·0. In both cases a coefficient of ·95 was calculated.

VALIDITY. The validity of the test was investigated by correlating the test results with those of the Terman Merrill. Three groups of children were used:

55 8-year-olds	correlation	·843
84 Backward 9-year-olds	correlation	·884
91 E.S.N. children from 11 to 16	correlation	·86

What should be in the test manual?

Due largely to the influence of Moray House and the N.F.E.R., test authors are now giving much more information about their tests than they did previously. The standards of test manuals will continue to rise as teachers become better informed, and more critical and demanding of publishers. A good test manual should contain detailed information on the following points. If it does not, the the author of the test may be willing to supply it.

1. The purpose of the test and how the results from it can best be used.
2. How to give the test, mark it, and interpret the results.
3. Details about the subjects on whom the test was standardised, their age, sex, numbers, geographical area, etc.
4. Reliability and validity data.
5. A summary of the contents of the test.
6. Reference to articles, books, etc., which may give further relevant information about the test and its use.
7. Date of standardisation.

3

Using and Misusing Tests

Coaching and practice

Before discussing the place of coaching and practice in the use of standardised tests, the difference between the two should be clear. If a child were given a test, then given one very similar to it, the first could be described as practice for the second. But if answers on the first were discussed, mistakes pointed out, underlying principles made clear, then the child could be said to have been coached for the second test. Coaching helps the child to gain insight into the problems, to learn the most efficient ways of tackling them; it is a course in testmanship. Practice, on the other hand, consists of allowing the child to work a few items similar to those in the proposed test, to familiarize him with the general layout and give a mental 'set' towards the test.

Research findings by Yates[1] and by Vernon[2] leave no doubt that mental ability scores can be raised by a period of practice or coaching. This does not mean that real intelligence is thereby increased. All that the child has really done is to learn a little more about how to do a specific task under very circumscribed conditions.

In the heyday of the eleven plus there was widespread coaching and practice both by schools and by private tutors. But research showed that there was a limit to the increase in test scores resulting from such preparation, and in an attempt to frustrate the efforts of over-ambitious and misguided parents and teachers, the practical suggestion was made that a period of coaching or practice should be given to all children intending to take the eleven plus examination.

[1] *Brit. J. Educ. Psych.*, No. 23, 1953.
[2] *Brit. J. Educ. Pysch.*, No. 24, 1954.

Only a minority of local authorities adopted this idea, but it has become very common indeed for standardised tests to include in the test booklet a number of items to be gone through with the tester before the actual test is given. Many of the Cotswold Tests, for example have a complete page of practice items on the back of the test booklet. Where practice items are provided, they should be used exactly as the author directs, for these are part of the standardised procedure.

Teaching the test

The gravest misuse to which tests can be put to is to use the actual items as lesson material. This misuse applies more commonly to attainment tests. Is it genuinely believed that by deliberately teaching ten words on, say, the Schonell Graded Word Test, that a child's real reading age is thereby increased by one year? Yet the practice exists. Such test-teaching is based upon a misunderstanding of two basic principles of test construction:

1. Test items are only a sample, they are valuable not so much for their intrinsic nature as for what they represent in terms of many other items of similar difficulty.
2. A child's test result is only valid if the child has been taught under very much the same conditions as were those with whom he is being compared, i.e. the standardisation sample.

Regarding the first of these principles, the forty words of a reading test which may represent a reading age of nine years are obviously not the only words of that level the child with a reading age of nine knows, but are a sample scientifically chosen to represent many hundreds of words. To teach a child only the words of the test, without his having the large reading vocabulary of children who read such words without being coached, is like teaching the answers to an examination instead of working through the syllabus first.

As regards the second principle, since the children on whom the test was standardised were not coached, then any score by a coached child must by definition be invalid.

It may be that the standardised test is looked upon with such awe that it is mistakenly believed to contain what *ought* to be taught. But this is standing education on its head. It is for the school to make its own syllabus according to its own lights. As we have seen in an earlier section the test-maker is not primarily concerned with what should be taught. He accepts the advice of the teachers on this matter. He concerns himself with the technique of measurement, with making more objective and reliable the comparison of children's abilities.

Far from providing an ideal to be aimed at, standardised tests may be unsuitable for certain schools. The very fact that they are usually based on what is commonly achieved and taught, both in content and in sequence of presentation, makes them unsuitable for schools whose syllabus and general aims are different from the majority. Only if the school wishes to compare itself with a group outside the school say with the rest of the town or country, is a standardised test necessary.

The content of any school test should be consonant with the true aim of the school. One of the worst evils of the eleven plus examination was the backwash which resulted when some head teachers abandoned their own principles, yielded to the clamour of parents and came perilously close to 'teaching the test'.

Once the true nature of a standardised test is understood the test itself become more reliable, because the user will be at one with the author of the test, appreciating his difficulties, his aims, and co-operating fully by maintaining during testing the conditions which are necessary for the test to serve its proper function.

Keeping to the rules

While the number of teachers who actually teach the contents of tests must be very small, many more are probably guilty of misplaced generosity during the testing session. Most test manuals contain instructions such as: 'It is essential that the procedure here outlined should be followed exactly. No deviation, however small, from the oral instruction is permissible.' But despite these warnings from a test author anxious that all his work shall not be brought to nought, human nature insists on breaking through. Some teachers find it almost impossible to keep to the instructions, especially when

19

testing their own pupils. For example, when it is found that the practice items are easy they are sometimes hurried over; but this can only be at the expense of the duller children. Despite instructions to the contrary the teacher may find it impossible to resist answering a seemingly innocent question. If towards the end of the test she sees that some items are very difficult (as is often the case, to give scope to the brilliant child) she may feel tempted to allow a few more minutes over the permitted time. These are deliberate infringements which should never occur. Just as important are the offences of which the testers are often not aware; the way they behave while the class is working, distracting pupils by talking with colleagues, moving about obtrusively or breathing down necks. It helps if the tester sees that he or she is part of the standardised conditions just as much as is the spacing of the desks and the timing.

Reproducing a published test

Tests are often misused by being reproduced. Quite apart from the infringement of copyright it is rare that the reproduction is made faithfully. The size of the print, spacing, detail of illustration, general layout, are all part of the standardised conditions that ought to obtain when the test is given. But it is regrettably easy to find, for example, a reading test which in its original version used several different sizes of print to cater for children of different ages, reproduced on an ordinary typewriter and given willy-nilly to children of all ages; or a picture test reproduced with nothing like the clarity of the original; or an arithmetic test written in indifferent figures on a poorly-lit blackboard.

For some children these changes may mean very little in terms of test scores; to others they will mean a lot. To the tester, it should matter that the test is not being given in conditions similar to those which obtained when the test was standardised.

How often should standardised tests be given?

Although this question is frequently asked it is impossible to quote a programme that will fit all cases. In a classifying school testing goes on more or less all the time; for special-school children there are scrupulous initial tests; in junior schools there will probably be yearly tests of attainment to obtain data for possible regrouping and to build up a cumulative picture of long-term progress; in the secondary school, in addition to the yearly attainment tests, tests of special aptitudes may be given to pick out children suited for special courses.

If there is one clear principle to fit all these situations it is that a test should be given only when there is a clear need for it and a prospect of acting upon the results.

Some teachers feel that there is too much testing. This is often a consequence of having to fill in yearly and perhaps termly reports on record cards which never seem to be used except for this purpose. It may be that such teachers do not stay in the school long enough to see the information used; nevertheless it is a good principle to try to ensure that when a teacher gives a test she is enabled to use the results. If the results are not usable then there has been no point in giving the test.

An antipathy towards testing may also arise from too close contact with a test-addict. Such addiction occurs most frequently among those who have recently discovered the riches of test literature and rush excitedly from one test to another, confident that the next will provide the perfect diagnosis or the ideal assessment; then as disillusion sets in, the malady fades. Permanent test-mania is much more serious: the sufferer appears to have rejected the belief that true education is a matter of excited exploration, a joint adventure for teacher and pupil, and prefers instead to peep at children through a secret spyhole, making contact with children only to measure them.

On the other hand there are those who are convinced that their own school does not test enough, where the business of the school appears to be to cover the syllabus and little attempt is made to check how the pupils interpret the teacher's words, or to diagnose possible learning difficulties. This is a matter of appreciating how children learn, a matter of deciding whether the school is going to be teacher-centred or child-centred.

Tests are but tools, to be used with discretion to serve the ultimate purpose of the school.

Should parents be told their child's I.Q.?

This question has a close affinity to 'Should children be told about sex?' and the answer is much the same; they should be told as much as they can understand and can 'take'. While a few parents may know more about the meaning of an I.Q. than the teacher, the majority will probably be under the impression that it is unalterable. In considering whether to divulge an I.Q. it is advisable to know something about the parent. What is his or her reaction likely to be on being told the child's I.Q.? The parent has every right to know what are the capabilities of his child; but will an I.Q. give this? The first duty of the teacher is to make sure that she herself understands the limitations of an I.Q. figure, its margin of error, its predictive value at particular ages, the wide difference between so-called 'intelligence' tests. The teacher who understands this will probably decide for herself that a much better way of informing parents about their child's capabilities and potential is to give an overall picture of the child; his strengths and weaknesses, his social as well as intellectual qualities. This information needs to be given in such a way that the child is compared with the rest of the school, and with the whole range of children of his age. As to the child's future, especially as regards older children, concrete examples based upon the careers of other similar children will be the most telling, stressing the wide range of occupations held by people of very similar scholastic records.

In other words, the child is presented not as a number but as a personality, with varied achievements and interests, and compared with children of his own age. The short answer to the question heading this section is that a full school report, supported by an interview with the teacher, can be far more informative, helpful and accurate than a mere I.Q. figure.

4

Testing Mental Ability

The term 'intelligence quotient' a misnomer

Although scores obtained from the mental-ability tests used in schools are often called intelligence quotients, this term is a misnomer. Firstly, if by intelligence is meant a general mental ability, the tests which are used in schools measure only one aspect of intelligence, an aspect which would be better described as 'scholastic ability'. Secondly, modern tests usually give results in terms of standard scores[1] rather than literal quotients. The word 'quotient' is often used to describe these scores but this practice is merely a legacy from the days when learning rates were calculated by using the formula:[2]

$$\frac{\text{Mental age}}{\text{Life age}} \times 100$$

to obtain what is referred to as a 'classical' I.Q.

Nowadays the word 'intelligence' is rarely used to describe tests of mental ability for use in schools. It was because test-users were apt to read more into the word than was intended, that the N.F.E.R. and Moray House dropped it from their test titles and adopted more cautious descriptions such as Verbal Reasoning Test, Picture Test and Non-Verbal Test.

The mental ability score as an average

It is a myth that the dull child excels with his hands, and that

[1] Standard scores are described on page 34.
[2] For speedy calculations of this formula, see *Tweeddale I.Q. Conversion Tables*, Oliver and Boyd.

weakness in one direction is compensated by strength in another. Teachers will confirm that the child poor at one thing is usually poor at most; the child bright in one subject is usually bright in others. Certainly there are children with outstanding single talents but the very fact that these excite comment shows their rarity.

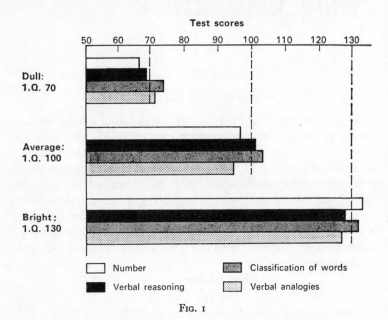

Fig. 1

This general principle, observable both in the day-to-day life of the school and in the results of objective tests, suggest that there is a certain quality which enters into each person's every mental activity, the magnitude of which marks that person's general level of mental ability or 'intelligence'. When one considers the diverse social, physical, emotional and intellectual qualities that may contribute towards intelligent behaviour, there are obviously a great number and variety of items that might be considered for a place in a test of all-round ability. But as the maker of school tests is concerned to measure only ability for school work, the tests he devises are limited to that area. Perhaps it is because some teachers have mistaken a narrow scholastic ability for general mental ability that they have been astonished when children whose school record had been only mediocre, later reached high levels of achievement as they moved into situations where those talents which had remained untapped at school were recognised and rewarded.

Tests of scholastic ability usually include subtests of different kinds, e.g. reasoning with numbers, reasoning with words, classifying words, understanding analogies, and each child's subtest scores usually cluster around a certain level. This general level is what is indicated by an I.Q. The figure above shows typical test profiles based on a scholastic-ability test consisting of four subtests. The scores for a dull, average and bright child, can be seen to cluster around the levels of 70, 100 and 130 points respectively.

In Figure 1 above the scale starts at 50 because children who score below this are usually unsuitable for ordinary school.

The growth of mental ability

Those who give tests of mental ability and wish to interpret the results wisely must know something of the nature and growth of what they are testing. In the foreword to the Newsom Report, Sir Edward Boyle made a statement that aroused much controversy: 'The essential point is that all children should have an equal opportunity to *acquire* intelligence and of developing their talents to the full.' The italics are mine. Despite objections at the time, there is little doubt that Boyle did not overstate the case when he used the word 'acquire', if by intelligence he did not mean Hebb's intelligence A, an innate unmeasurable potential, but Intelligence B, which is the developed ability to think intelligently. Within the limits determined by the nature of the inherited genes, mental ability can be acquired. It is now taken for granted that mental ability develops as a result of the constant interaction between the child and its environment, and there are an increasing number of researches directed at teasing out some of the factors chemical, biological, neurological, social, emotional that may influence the growing intellect.

We know that genes inherited at conception determine certain physical characteristics such as eye colour, blood group and hair texture which environment can do little to change. But how far

25

genes determine the growth of intellect is still a matter for research. Evidence of a strong genetic influence seems to be provided by, on the one hand generations of dull children from the same stock, on the other, brilliant families such as the Huxleys and the Darwins. But the issue is not so simple. Closer examination of such cases reveals that the dull children have often been reared in depressing slum conditions while the brilliant families have enjoyed a highly stimulating childhood. Goddard's theory that criminality and subnormality were inherited traits has been shown to have much less validity than was claimed. His book[1] which told the story of how a soldier in the American Civil War had children by a feeble-minded woman and by a woman of normal intelligence thus becoming the ancestor of two distinct lines of descendants, the one 'prominent people in all walks of life' and the other composed of 'paupers, criminals, prostitutes, drunkards', received considerable support at the time of publication but has long since been shown to be too dependent on hearsay and to have ignored the possible influences of environment.

Knowing as much as we do about the permanency of those attitudes to learning that are formed in infancy, and about the influence of social class upon the types of education children obtain[2] it seems reasonable to suggest that teachers should pay great respect to the claims of environmental influence; not least because they, in their speech, attitudes, and ideals, are part of that influence.

Attempts have been made to study the interaction of nature and nurture by comparing the mental ability scores of related and unrelated children. The scores, given below, at first glance suggest a predominating influence of heredity.

Degree of Relationship	Correlation between I.Q.s
Unrelated children	0·0
Siblings, reared together	·5
Fraternal twins, reared together	·5
Identical twins, reared together	·9

But it may be objected that the correlation between the scores of the related children may be largely influenced by environment, because

[1] H. H. Goddard, *The Kallikak Family*, Macmillan, 1912.
[2] B. Jackson and J. Marsden, *Education and the Working Class*, Routledge, 1962.

being reared together would give these children very similar levels of social and educational experiences. This would be even more the case with twins who by virtue of their age would actually share a great many experiences, and at the time of the intelligence testing would be at the same level of physical development (a factor which has been shown[1] to affect mental development).

To observe the respective efforts of environment and heredity in the case of identical twins, an experiment that comes readily to mind is one in which the twins are separated early in life, allowed to grow up in quite different environments, then after a number of years are compared for mental ability. Since they come from the same egg and share the same set of genes, any difference in their ultimate level of ability might be ascribed to the effects of environment.

This theory was investigated by Newman, Freeman and Holzinger in a study[2] of nineteen identical twins separated early in life. These twins were observed as adults and it was found that those pairs who had been reared in sharply-differing environments showed clear differences in mental-ability scores, differences which appeared to be related to educational oportunities. The general concensus o opinion on the relative influences of heredity and environment is that the genes set the upper limit of development, but how far and in which directions development proceeds depends upon the way in which the organism reacts to the demand of the environment. A more homely illustration is that every person is dealt a hand, but how he plays it depends upon how he reacts to the cards played by others in the game.

The power of genetic influence can be seen in children who, despite our most strenuous efforts, never rise above the level of subnormality; and conversely in socially underprivileged children who show from early childhood a constant superiority of intellect. At any point in time the extent of a person's mental ability will be determined by (a) the nature of his previous experiences, and (b) how far his innate ability has allowed him to profit from those experiences. This 'ability to profit' should not be seen as an unalterable quality but one which, as the next section shows, may change as the result of experience.

[1] See *Education and Physical Growth* by J. Tanner, U.L.P.
[2] *Twins: A Study of Heredity and Environment*, University of Chicago Press, 1937.

Fluctuation in intelligence-test scores

If the growth of mental ability is affected by experience we can expect that a person's successive test scores will fluctuate as his changing moods, attitudes, insights, influence his behaviour. A person's test scores may also vary because of imperfections in the test, or in the tester's technique.

The changes that occur in the same person's intelligence test scores over a number of years were investigated by Nancy Bayley[1] who tested at frequent intervals groups of children at various ages. The simplified table below is derived from her detailed findings and clearly shows that:

1. The test score of a child under six may be a poor predictor of his later test scores.
2. The longer the time between the two tests the lower is the correlation between the scores.
3. The older the child the more dependable will be his score for prediction purposes.

CORRELATION BETWEEN FIRST AND SUBSEQUENT I.Q.S.

| | *Correlation with initial I.Q.* | |
Age at first test	*1 year later*	*6 years later*
3 years	·64	·55
6 years	·86	·81
7 years	·88	·75
11 years	·93	·92

Changes in a person's mental-ability scores are the rule rather than the exception. Some writers have estimated that the average amount of change between the ages of seven and fifteen is within fairly narrow limits, about ten points either up or down. Just as his height/weight ratio follows a fairly predictable course unless disturbed by untoward events, so each child generally keeps within his 'track of mental development'.

But while mental ability scores for most people remain fairly

[1] *J. Genetic Psych.*, **75**, 1949.

stable there have been striking instances of 'track-changing' when changes of up to thirty points have been recorded. These have almost invariably been accompanied by equally dramatic changes in the personal circumstances of the subject. For example, Skeels and Dye[1] report increases of over forty points by orphans removed from a restrictive orphanage to affectionate homes; Clarke and Clarke[2] report increases of up to twenty-seven points by sub-normal adults removed from 'adverse environments' to hospital care; and programmes of remedial education given to 'culturally deprived' Negro and Puerto Rican students in New York are reported[3] to have produced striking increases in individual intelligence test scores.

These cases support the view that a test of mental ability is not a test of pure capacity, for in these cases the initial scores did not reveal the latent capacity, but a measure of what had been learned under certain circumstances: if previous experiences have been abnormal then the test result may reflect them and be misinterpreted as a measure indicating true capacity.

In judging whether a child's mental ability is fluctuating sufficiently to cause concern one needs to consider the following factors: the type of test used, the reliability of test and testers, the period of time between tests and the age of the child. As will be seen in Part Two, 'intelligence' tests vary widely in their content, some requiring reading ability, some only an understanding of oral instructions, some the manipulation of objects, and others the solving of pattern-puzzles. Test-score changes do not necessarily mean real changes in the ability of the person tested.

Relationship between mental ability and attainment

In the figure on page 24 it can be seen that the I.Q. is an average of several subtest scores. It suffers from the defect of every average in that it represents in only a general way the separate scores from which it is derived. It is lower than some and higher than others. Now if a child is given a test on the topic of only one of these sub-tests, say verbal reasoning or number, it can be expected that the

[1] *Proc. Amer. Assoc. Mental Deficiency*, **44**, 1939.
[2] *Brit. J. Psych.*, **45**, 1954.
[3] M. Mayer, *The Schools*, Bodley head, 1961.

result may be higher or lower than his I.Q. This is not surprising since a mental ability test is measuring what is common to many different types of mental processes, whereas an attainment test measures a more specific ability. The clinching argument against those who assume that a child's attainment score should be almost identical with his mental ability score is that the facts deny it. Any class taken at random will be found to contain many children whose subject quotients are up to ten points higher or lower than their intelligence quotients. Unless the discrepancy is fifteen points or more it should not be considered particularly significant.

One should regard with suspicion any figures that purport to show that a child is under-achieving or over-achieving unless they are accompanied by detailed information about the kind of tests used. As we shall see in the following pages there are wide variations between tests which are supposed to be measuring the same thing. A crude comparison of scores is an unrewarding exercise unless the tests have been closely matched for the scatter of their scores and and for the type of children on whom they were standardised. It would be quite wrong, for example, to use as evidence of retardation or advancement the difference between scores on the Burt Graded Word Reading Test and on the Stanford-Binet Intelligence Scale, without taking into account that the former is based upon the performance of Scottish children in the 1930s and the latter on American children in the 1950s.

When a child's attainment score is much lower than his mental-ability score teachers tend to accept this without a qualm as indicating retardation. But when the discrepancy is the other way round there is often an uneasy feeling that something is wrong with the tests. This confusion arises from the mistaken view that a test of mental ability is a measure of capacity on all subjects.

There is no absolute difference between intelligence and attainment tests. 'What do we mean by the word "pity"?' and 'Give me six blocks' could appear in both intelligence and attainment tests. On the whole, intelligence tests involve thinking techniques that can be applied to a wide variety of problems: analogies and classification problems are good examples of this kind of thinking. Attainment tests measure skills that have been deliberately taught in school, specific skills such as the division of fractions and parts of speech.

Giving meaning to a score

Raw scores, i.e. the actual marks earned on the test, are of some little use in that they will allow crude comparisons between scores, or enable progress to be measured on the same test. But they do not lend themselves to comparisons between tests since the same raw score on different tests may have quite different values. The more common methods of making raw scores more meaningful include the use of (1) age-units, (2) quotients, (3) percentiles and (4) standard scores.

Age units

Converting a raw score to an age unit involves relating it to the average score made by children of a certain age: thus a twelve-year-old who makes the same score as the average eight-year-old would be credited with a mental or attainment age of eight. The use of mental ages and attainment ages has its weaknesses. One is that the word 'age' may be taken to imply more than it should, e.g. a ten-year-old with a mental age of fourteen may be expected to behave in all respects like a fourteen-year-old, or a ten-year-old with a reading age of six may be expected to learn to read on books written for six-year-olds.

Another weakness is that the age-steps may not be of equal value, i.e. the increase in difficulty between say the six- and the seven-year levels may not be the same as that between the ten- and the eleven-year levels. Another difficulty arises when age units are used as absolute measures of retardation or advancement, since a retardation of two years in an eight-year-old gives a quotient of 75 ($\frac{6}{8} \times$ 100) while a two years' retardation in a sixteen year-old gives a quotient of $87\frac{1}{2}$ ($\frac{14}{16} \times$ 100).

Some of the weaknesses of the age-unit method also affect the use of quotients, since quotients are based upon age units. The chief value of quotients is that they indicate *rate* of learning.

Percentiles

A simple way of comparing a child's score with those of the rest of the group is by the use of percentiles. This simply means arranging the set of scores in order of merit, then fitting this rank order to a range of 0 to 100. The child whose score is better than 10 per cent of the group is given a percentile rank of 10, the child whose score is better than 50 per cent of the group is given a percentile rank of 50, the child whose score is better than 75 per cent of the group is given a percentile rank of 75 and so on. Percentile ranks can be used with any kind of group whether the children are all of low or high ability; but when the group to be tested is representative of the whole range of ability, then percentiles can be used in a special way to give 'standard scores'.[1]

Scatter

The use of standard scores (or deviation scores as they are sometimes called) depends upon the assumption that mental and scholastic ability is distributed among the general population in a particular way, and upon the test being constructed to suit this distribution of ability. The advantages of using such specially constructed tests can be appreciated by considering the snags that arise when comparing the same raw score made on tests that differ considerably in the scatter of their scores.

If Johnny tells his parents that he has been given six marks on an arithmetic test, a likely reply might be: 'What did the others get?' If Johnny says that the average was ten, does the value of six become any clearer? Not much, for as may be seen in the two sets of scores below, a score of six in Test 1 is the nearest to the average, but a score of six in Test 2 is farther from the average than most.

Test 1	1	3	4	6	10 av	15	16	17	18
Test 2	6	7	8	9	10	11	12	13	14

It can be seen that the value of a particular score depends not simply upon how much it is above or below the average, but upon how that difference compares with the differences between the average and each of the other scores. Now if it can be arranged that all tests are so scored that they have the same average, and produce the same scatter of scores above and below that average, then it

---

[1] See p. 153 for such a conversion table.

becomes possible to compare scores on each of these tests straight off, since the same score made on any of the tests has exactly the same value relative to the rest of the scores. This is how most modern tests are constructed. British test-makers have agreed to call the average score on each test a hundred. The way in which the scores are scattered above and below that average bears a close resemblance to the pattern of differences that shows itself when a cross-section of the population is measures for certain attributes, i.e. in a 'normal distribution'.

The normal distribution

If we took all the children of one age group in a city and measured their feet, their weights, their speed at running a hundred yards, then put the scores for each test in rank order, each set of scores would show very much the same kind of pattern. This pattern is shown in Figure 2, with most of the scores close to the average, and the number of instances diminishing as the lower and higher extremes are approached. This kind of dispersion appears to be a natural law which operates wherever a great many chance factors are present.

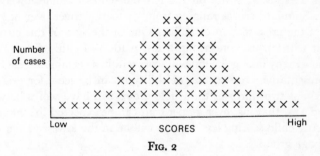

Fig. 2

Mathematicians have based upon it an ideal curve, the curve of normal distribution, which has some very useful properties especially in matters that concern predicting the odds for or against an event happening by chance. On the assumption that mental qualities are distributed in this way, the test-maker constructs his test and its scoring so that the results conform to this 'normal curve'. Of course

33

if such a standardised test were to be given to a single class or a small school the results would probably not show this symmetrical pattern because the numbers would be too small to include the full range of ability. But if a big cross-section of children were used, say a city's population, an approximate normal curve would result. Figure 3 shows this normal distribution.

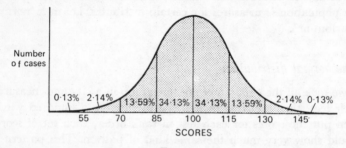

FIG. 3

In Figure 3 the numbers along the base line are 'standard scores'. It can be seen that the middle score is 100 (this is also the average score since the curve is symmetrical) and on the right the scores get higher and fewer, while on the left the scores become lower and fewer. Standard scores ranging from 55 to 145 cover over 99½ per cent of the cross-section of ability. One of the uses of this curve is that it will tell us, concerning a test made to fit this distribution, just how many taking the test will score within a certain range. Given a representative cross-section of ability it can be seen, for example that about two-thirds of the whole group will have scores between 85 and 115, that just over 2½ per cent can be expected to score over 130. Any child scoring less than 70 will be in the lowest 2½ per cent of his age group.

The choice of 100 as the middle or average score is quite arbitrary. Some tests, usually American, use 50 as the average score.

How a conversion table is made

In most test manuals there is a table which enables the tester to convert a child's raw score to a standard score. A word or two

34

about the construction of this kind of table will lead to a more confident use of it.

When the test-maker is standardising his test, he collects all the test papers completed by the children on whom the test is being standardised and arranges them first in age sets, i.e. all those by children aged 9 years 1 month together, all those by children aged 9 years 2 months together, etc., and then each age set is put in order of merit.

The raw scores in each set are then 'fitted' to a normal distribution, i.e. the middle score is given a standard score of 100, the top $2\frac{1}{2}$ per cent are given scores of above 130, the bottom $2\frac{1}{2}$ per cent given scores of under 70, and all the scores in between are allotted appropriate standard scores according to where they fall in the percentage distribution shown in Figure 3 above. In this way each child's score is compared with those of his own age group and one can see at a glance how much he is above or below the average for his age.

Table 1 is an example of such a conversion table. In the column of scores for 10-year-olds we can see that a raw score of 47 represents a standardised score of 100: the same score made by a child aged 10.9 would represent a standardised score of only 87 which is very much below average for that age group.

Standard scores, therefore, show how a child compares with his own age group. They do not compare him with children of other ages, as mental-age scores may do.

Some people find it easier to think in percentages rather than in terms of standard scores. To change a raw score into percentiles using Table 1:

1. Along the top line find the age of the child, say 10.6 years.
2. Look down that column to find the child's score, say 64.
3. Move along that row to the extreme right where the figure in the percentile column is 75. This means that the $10\frac{1}{2}$-year-old who scores 64 has a higher score than 75 per cent of all the $10\frac{1}{2}$-year-olds. It does not mean that the child has got 75 per cent of the available marks.

In using percentiles, however, one needs to be aware that the units are of unequal value. By looking at the 50th and 60th percentile raw scores, for any one age, e.g. 61 and 65 in the 11-year-old column, it can be seen that the difference is only 3 or 4 points. But between the 95th and 98th percentiles the difference in raw scores is sometimes as high as 12 points. One should not, therefore, add percentile scores from one test to those derived from another to find a total or an average, as one can with standard scores.

TABLE I. EXAMPLE OF A CONVERSION TABLE

Standard scores	Ages in years and months								Percentiles
	9.3	9.6	9.9	10.0	10.3	10.6	10.9	11.0	
140	99	103	107	110	114	116	117	118	
135	85	89	92	97	97	100	105	106	
130	72	75	78	81	84	87	90	93	98
125	60	63	67	70	75	76	80	83	95
120	57	60	64	67	70	73	77	81	90
113	53	55	58	61	64	67	70	74	80
110	48	52	55	58	61	64	68	70	75
108	46	50	53	56	59	62	66	68	70
104	42	45	48	51	54	58	62	65	60
100	35	42	44	47	51	54	58	61	50
96	34	37	39	43	48	52	56	58	40
92	31	34	36	40	44	48	53	55	30
90	39	31	34	38	42	46	50	52	25
87	27	30	32	35	38	42	47	49	20
80	21	23	25	29	33	37	40	42	10
75	18	21	23	26	29	32	36	38	5
70	9	12	14	16	19	21	25	27	2
65	1	2	3	4	5	7	9	14	

The relationship between standard scores and percentiles[1]

By putting a scale of standard scores against a percentile scale, a simple conversion can be made. In Table 2 it can be seen that if, for example, a child made a score at the 75th percentile on the Raven's Matrices test (which gives scores only in percentiles) this would be equivalent to an I.Q. of 110; a percentile score of 5 would be equivalent to a standard score of 75, and so on.

[1] See Appendix for a full table relating percentile scores to standard scores.

TABLE 2. RELATIONSHIP BETWEEN STANDARD SCORES AND
PERCENTILE SCORES

Standard scores	70	75	80	85	90	100	110	115	120	125	130
Approx. percentile scores	2	5	10	16	25	50	75	84	90	95	98

The standard deviation

Another way of expressing a test score is in terms of standard deviations. It was noted above that a score can be given meaning by saying how much it differs from the average compared with the differences between the average and all the other scores. Roughly speaking the standard deviation is the average amount by which all the separate scores differ from the average, i.e. it is a measure of dispersion or scatter. British test-makers have agreed to make the standard deviation of their tests scores 15 points.

In Figure 3, p. 34, it will be seen that the intervals along the base line are of 15 points. A standard score of 115 could be described as one standard deviation above the average, or +1 S.D. A standard score of 85 would be described as −1 S.D. Expressed in this way, a score gives an immediate indication of how it differs from the average compared with all the other scores. Such scores are sometimes called sigma scores, after the Greek letter s. The relationship between sigma scores and standard scores may be seen below:

Standard scores	55	70	85	100	115	130	145
Sigma scores	−3	−2	−1	0	+1	+2	+3

For scores that are between these units of 15 points, fractions of 15 are used. Thus a standardised score of 133 would be +2·2, because 33 is 2 times 15 plus two-tenths of 15. To work out the standard deviation for any set of figures, see the worked example in the Appendix.

Table for relating percentile scores to standard scores

Three kinds of test scores related to the normal curve of distribution are shown below. These scores and the kind of conversion table on

37

page 36 can be used for any kind of test, whether attainment or mental ability, as long as the test has been made to give a normal distribution of scores with a mean of 100 and an S.D. of 15.

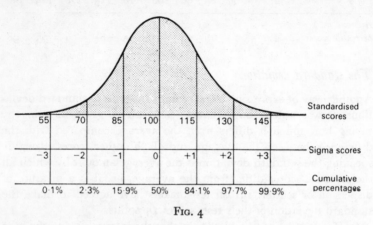

FIG. 4

Standard error of measurement (S.E.m.)

If a child is given a standardised test several times within a short period of time, his scores will probably vary within a narrow range. Thus any single administration will produce a score that may not be the child's true score but will be fairly near it. For any particular

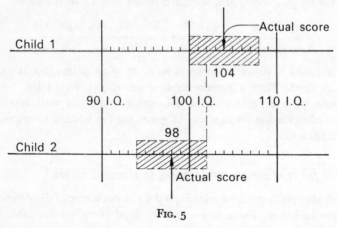

FIG. 5

test it is possible to calculate how much one needs to allow for errors intrinsic to the test situation. This figure is called the standard error of measurement. The larger this is, the less important will be a few points of difference between the scores of two children. For example, in the figure above the shaded area indicates the standard error, which in this case is plus or minus 4 points. It can be seen that although Child 1 has a higher actual score than Child 2, in fact Child 2 may have a higher true score than Child 1.

5

Current Trends in Intelligence Testing

The tests of mental ability used in schools and clinics today have been criticised on the grounds that they fail to detect certain kinds of talent which often prove of great value in post-school life. Conventional tests are of obvious use in that, within limits, they do the job for which they are intended: to select children for particular courses of education. But what they fail to do, it is alleged, is to identify the creative thinkers, the original minds, the children who in later life startle society with their innovations.

The type of thinking measured by present intelligence tests is largely what has come to be called convergent thinking. This is the kind of mental process in which ideas, facts, relationships are organised in such a way as to lead to certain specified solutions. Since the tests contain tasks to which there is only one solution, the tested pupil must either fail or succeed. The convergent thinker makes progress by the skill with which he can criticise and dismiss hypotheses that appear unsuitable. He thinks cautiously and with economy.

The opposite type of thinking, described as divergent, is the kind in which, instead of following routine procedures, there is a questing, ready-for-anything attitude untrammelled by any mental 'set'. The divergent thinker is explorative, and constructive. In the true sense of the word he 'plays' with ideas, following intuition rather than logic, and is more likely than the convergent thinker to produce novel and original ideas.

One cannot, of course, blame the test-makers for not producing tests of creativity. Tests are made in response to the demands of the schools and if the majority of schools foster conforming attitudes then the test-makers are obliged to construct tests that measure conforming and conservative thinking. Until recently there appeared to be an unwritten assumption that the teacher knew all the 'right' answers and it was the pupil's job to learn those particular answers. The school was thought of as the store-house of final truths to be passed on to the diligent and the conforming. But now the fashionable words are 'discovery', 'open-ended' and 'creativity', and test-makers are being asked to produce tests which will detect the creative thinkers.

Tests of creativity

Can we test creativity? Although there are not yet any fully-validated tests of creativity there have been some interesting experiments. A pioneer in the identification of creative processes of thought is Professor J.P. Guilford of Southern California. Some of Guilford's tests have featured open-ended questions, to which there are no cut-and-dried answers, responses being evaluated according to their degree of originality and ingenuity. Whereas the convergent thinker responds to such questions with dignified acceptable answers, the divergent thinker gives answers that are often impossible and bizarre.

Getzels and Jackson have described[1] how they followed Guilford's lead and tried to identify children who were both intelligent and creative. Their tentative tests of creativity included asking pupils to invent a story to fit a simple picture. Typical stories about a man in an aeroplane were:

High I.Q. subject

'Mr Smith is on his way home after a successful business trip. He is very happy and is thinking about his wonderful family and how glad he will be to see them again. He can picture it, about an hour from now, his plane landing at the airport and Mrs Smith and their three children all welcoming him home.'

High creative subject

'This man is flying back from Reno where he has won a divorce from his wife. He could not stand to live with her any more, he told

[1] J. W. Getzels and P. W. Jackson, *Creativity and Intelligence*, Wiley, 1962.

the judge, because she wore so much cold cream on her face at night that her head would skid across the pillow and hit him in the head. He is now contemplating a new skid-proof face cream.'

Getzels and Jackson found that the group they identified as creative thinkers were, compared with other children:

1. Less concerned with scholastic success.
2. Less favoured by teachers.
3. Less apt to accept the teacher as a model to be copied.
4. Interested in a wider range of subjects.
5. Richer in their sense of humour.

A later work[1] by Wallach and Kogan suggested that tests of creativity should not be obvious test situations, as they were in the experiments by Getzels and Jackson. The lives of truly creative people, it was held, showed that the necessary conditions for creative thinking included (a) an absence of external pressure and (b) a playful, gamelike attitude to the problem. Thus in, Wallach and Kogan's experiments the word 'test' was not used, no writing was required, unlimited time was allowed, and a permissive attitude encouraged. Examples of the 'games' used were:

1. ALTERNATE USES. The child was asked to say in how many different ways certain common objects could be used, e.g. a newspaper, knife, cork.

2. PATTERN MEANINGS. A number of patterns were presented and the child asked to mention all the things each pattern reminded him of.

3. INSTANCES. The child was asked to name all the things he could think of that were, e.g. round, square, made a noise, moved on wheels.

A child's creativity was measured by (a) the total number of responses he gave, and (b) the uniqueness of his responses. Some unique answers were:
Alternate uses. A tyre . . . grow tomatoes in it.

[1] Wallach M. A. and Kogan N., *Modes of Thinking in Young Children*, Holt Rinehart and Winston. 1965.

Instances. A thing that makes a noise . . . . snoring; a cash register.
Pattern meanings.

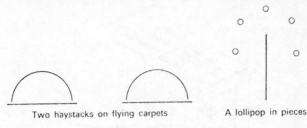

Two haystacks on flying carpets   A lollipop in pieces

FIG. 6

Guilford's model of intelligence

Guilford's experiments concerning the nature of creativity were only
part of an attempt to build a general theory of intelligence. The
basis of this theory is that each mental ability has three aspects, i.e.
content, process and product. Each of these aspects may take a
variety of forms. The *content* of a particular type of ability might be
one of four kinds:

(a) Symbolic, e.g. letters, numbers or other conventional signs.
(b) Figural, e.g. material that is non-representational.
(c) Semantic, e.g. material in the form of verbal meanings.
(d) Behavioural, e.g. social behaviour.

The *process* involved in a particular ability may be one of five
kinds, i.e. convergent thinking, divergent thinking, memorisation,
cognition, evaluation.

The *product* of an act of thinking might be one of six kinds:

(a) Units, e.g. lists of words or items.
(b) Classes, e.g. classification of words, pictures.
(c) Relations, e.g. as in analogies.
(d) Systems, e.g. an overall pattern of meaning.
(e) Transformations, e.g. visualising a plan as a made-up object.
(f) Implications, e.g. foreseeing possible consequences.

To illustrate how these dimensions of thought relate to each other Guilford has suggested as a model the kind of cube shown below.[1]

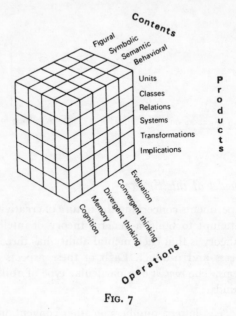

FIG. 7

Each of the smaller cubes is a unique combination of kinds of operation, content, and product. This is best illustrated by taking a typical item from an intelligence test and showing how it can be described in Guilford's terms.

Mary is darker than Ann.
Mary is fairer than Joan.
Who is fairer: Ann or Joan?

Here the content is clearly semantic, the operation or process is convergent thinking (since the result is determined), and the product is an implication.

An example from a possible test of creativity might be:

'Tell me all the things you can think of that are square?'

[1] From 'The Three Faces of Intellect', *The American Psychologist*, **14**, 1959.

Here the content is semantic, the process divergent thinking, and the products are units.

Guilford's model of the structure of the intellect is as yet theoretical, and all the 120 factors postulated here have not been operationally defined. Nevertheless the model has obvious implications for the maker of tests. It suggests that in order to detect a person's full resources a large number and a wide variety of tests will be needed. At least four kinds of intelligence must be allowed for: the concrete intelligence involved in using figural information; abstract intelligence, involving the use of symbols, especially in mathematics and languages; semantic intelligence, involving the understanding of verbal concepts; and social intelligence which concerns the abilities required in dealing with people. In isolating creativity, problems must be posed which allow the creative process to reveal itself operating on different kinds of content.

In this trend towards a finer and finer analysis of mental abilities it is clear that the single I.Q. figure of the past is giving way to the profile, the multiple assessment. This development is already foreshadowed in the design of the New British Intelligence Scale outlined in the next section.

The British Intelligence Scale

In September 1965 proposals were announced for a new British Intelligence Scale. For British psychologists and all concerned with mental measurement, this news was epoch-making. There has been for many years a wide variety of British intelligence tests, but none has been as thorough nor as reliable as the Stanford-Binet or the Wechsler, both of which are of American origin and have to be adapted for British use. To produce an intelligence test as valuable as the two mentioned above is an immense undertaking, lengthy and costly. A glance at the second chapter of Terman and Merrill's *Measuring Intelligence* gives some indication of the years of work, the selection and grading of items, the consideration given to social status and geographical area when selecting the standardisation samples, and the careful statistical analysis, that are involved in assembling an up-to-date nationally valid test of intelligence. When the British test is completed, possibly by 1974, it will probably supplant the Stanford-Binet and the Wechsler tests so far as Britain is concerned.

The scale will be standardised on children drawn from various social classes, rural and urban communities, and the main geographical areas of Great Britain. It will probably consist of 144 items and be designed to test the intelligence of children from five to twelve years. Except for the items for higher ages there will be no reading matter. Although the device of mental age will not be used, the range will extend in mental-age terms from about two to fifteen years.

It is expected that there will be twelve subscales to measure specialised abilities falling under the general headings of Reasoning, Number, Memory, Fluency, Verbal, and Spatial, with subscales, on for example, visual memory, auditory memory, vocabulary, information, comprehension and operational thinking.

Scoring may be expressed not only as a number but as a quality: in reasoning, for example, a child may be described as being able to think concretely, or intuitively, or in abstract terms. Each scaled score will be on a 1 to 100 scale but the overall score will be in the usual range for I.Q.s with 100 for the mean. Instead of a score being given as a single figure it is likely to be described as being within a certain band, covering a range of 10 points.

A test result will be presented in a way that shows the relative scores in each of the main ability scales.

The chief advantages of the new scale appear to be:

1. Scores obtained from this test, unlike those from the Stanford-Binet and Wechsler, will contain norms which are true for British children.
2. Expressing scores in bands rather than in single numbers avoids the ridiculous situation in which a child with an I.Q. of 99 may be considered inferior to a child with an I.Q. of 101.
3. The profile type of record will give a more useful and less ambiguous picture of a child's abilities than would a single I.Q. figure.
4. Since the test items explore thought processes hitherto ignored in many intelligence tests, this may lead to the detection of abilities and disabilities that may otherwise have gone unnoticed.

5. Results in terms of levels of thinking will give the educator useful guidelines in planning programmes for particular children.

Liaison between teacher and ascertainment officer

There is no doubt that the assessment of handicapped or problem children can only be done by someone with a thorough training in testing techniques and test interpretation. In the event, such assessments are often carried out by school medical officers whose psychological training has been a mere three weeks. The need for more educational psychologists is a problem that cries out for vigorous action, and while it is no concern of this book to press this case, it is certainly relevant to point to the need for intelligible and realistic reports from the testing officer to the teacher.

When a teacher asks for a child to be given a detailed intelligence test, she hopes to receive a diagnosis that is (*a*) written in plain English and (*b*) constructive in terms of actual school conditions. But she is sometimes disappointed.

Many of these reports, and recommendations for future treatment, are often made without prior consultation with the child's teacher, who may well have a wealth of knowledge about the child's behaviour in class, and can advise on what is or is not possible in the way of making special arrangements if the child is to remain in her class. While machinery for this kind of consultation is officially encouraged, in the event it is often ignored.

At one extreme is the report which appears to have been written by a psychiatrist communing with himself. At the other extreme are the oft-quoted cases, but mercifully occurring less and less, of the teacher who at her wit's end sends a child for assessment and eventually receives a report of the type:

> Mary Roberts was examined on the 5th November and was found to have an I.Q. of 79. She should receive special treatment in the ordinary school.

No mention is made of the kind of test used, the child's behaviour during the test, nor any suggestions as to what kind of special treatment should be given. This kind of report is written by someone who may well have learned to administer intelligence tests but to whom differential diagnosis and the wide variety of possible remedial treatment is a closed book.

An example of the kind of report for which teachers are extremely grateful is the following:

Peter was tested on the Wechsler Intelligence Scale. This scale gives an opportunity to compare verbal with practical and spatial ability. His Verbal score was 115 and his Performance (practical and spatial) score was 102. The variations in his development are shown by the disparities on the various subtests as well as by his behaviour during the interview. His intelligence has a marked verbal bias, he has a poor visual memory, a poor short-term aural memory, and limited concentration. His test scores should be regarded as a minimum in view of his immaturity in certain social respects.

His retardation, $1\frac{1}{2}$ years on the Schonell Problem Arithmetic Test and 1 year on the Neale Analysis of Reading Ability, is to some degree due to his social immaturity. His physical timidity may account for his verbal bias to some extent, and it would be wrong to allow his dislike of physical activity to strengthen this bias even further. He needs a firm hand, and the minimum of obvious special treatment.

Intellectually he is capable of working in your Commercial stream but one should not expect him to reach his full potential until puberty.

Here the teacher is told exactly which tests were used, how the boy performed on certain subtests, why the bare test figure may be misleading, what kind of discipline may be best, and where he could best fit into the organisation of that particular school. The report is clear, practical, and of positive help in the future treatment of the child in school.

In fairness it must be said that most psychological services for schools are grossly understaffed. The employment of school medical officers as testers of intelligence appears to be a necessity at the moment if all the ascertainment-work is to be coped with; but it is also an anomaly which must eventually be removed, if both the school medical service and the school psychological service are to serve their proper function. Certainly school medical officers need to keep themselves informed about educational psychology, just as educational psychologists must be aware of the influence of physical factors in the growth of intelligence. But in the assessment of a child's educational needs the recommendation that should carry most weight should surely be educational rather than medical. While it is true that many long-experienced chief school medical officers have a warm and informed understanding of the educational viewpoint, this cannot be said of a minority, nor is it always possible for them to supervise closely the intelligence-testing done by S.M.O.s who have only recently completed their brief mental-testing course.

The future of testing

A current proposal in the administrative field of education is the more extensive use of regionalism, i.e. the establishing of larger units of organisation. While regionalism has many obvious advantages, its value to the maker of tests has received scant notice. It has been shown in previous pages that an educational test standardised in area A will be invalid in area B in so far as the two areas differ in respect of those factors that may influence test performance, e.g. local vocabulary, social conditions, quality and type of teaching. For a small authority to produce tests specially suited to its own children the cost may well be prohibitive. But with the establishment of larger units of organisation, a local standardisation may well become easier to finance and to arrange, and the practice of having to give to the children of Rochdale tests which have been standardised in London will become less likely than in the past.

Test Libraries

Over the past few years the writer has asked successive groups of teachers attending courses of full-time further training how much they knew about educational tests, and the figures show that the average teacher had used no more than one standardised test and knew the names of no more than two others. Since there are, as this book shows, over 150 scholastic tests either available to teachers or featuring in reports which they may be expected to read during their daily work, there would seem to be some serious lack of communication.

49

There seems to be no reason why each local education authority should not have, and publicise, a well-stocked library of tests where teachers might browse and borrow just as they can in a public library. Possible locations for a test library are the L.E.A.'s teacher's library, the local Child Guidance Centre or the headquarters of the local remedial education service.

Courses on testing

For some readers the most important word in the previous section is 'publicise'. In other words, a good selection of tests may well be owned by a Schools Psychological Service or be in the care of a local Ascertainment Officer, but the prospect of making this common knowledge may not be welcome. There is some justification for this attitude, since even the simplest of standardised tests demands from those who give it an appreciation of the need to keep strictly to the instructions, to interpret the results sensibly, etc. But this fact should be seen not as a reason for keeping standardised tests as the preserve of psychologists and school medical officers, but as a reason for giving to more and more teachers the opportunity to learn how to administer educational tests. In the future every comprehensive school will need at least one member of the staff trained in the use of tests of achievement and ability in order to select children for courses, measure retardation, recommend for special educational treatment, etc.

Some teachers have already gained this skill by in-service courses arranged at the initiative of the local educational psychologist or by full-time courses at universities. But many more courses are needed. The content of these courses should not be as concentrated as that followed by a trainee educational psychologist but should be rigorous enough to entitle the holder of the course-award recognition by the N.F.E.R. as one who is allowed to use the P tests mentioned in Chapter 1. By multiplying the numbers of teachers who can use these tests one immediately releases the precious few educational psychologists we have from their burden of routine testing, enabling them to spend more time in lecturing and clinical work more worthy of their training and knowledge.

Resistance to the training of teachers in test-techniques often comes from those whose aim is not so much the improvement of our educational service as the preservation of status and a professional mystique.

Tests of creativity

While there are not yet any valid tests of creativity in this country the literature on this subject in the United States is now extremely impressive. It is only a matter of time before we are forced to take seriously the work of Torrance[1] and Guilford.[2] Even when tests of creativity have been evolved, there will still remain the basic problem of educating our teachers into accepting and fostering the creative child. It can be said at the moment that most teachers do not welcome deviational behaviour. Conformity is expected and encouraged. At the very least, tests of creativity may help teachers to recognise that the non-conforming child is not necessarily to be brought into line, that unusual and unexpected answers and solutions to problems should be treated with respect, that individual differences are the source of progress, and that there is a danger of submitting everything a child does to evaluation that reflects the worst of conservatism.

In the tests of creativity so far developed it appears that certain basic principles characterise the creative process regardless of the subject-content. By noting these basic principles teachers may be helped to identify creative thinking and performance in the classroom. When such creative children have been identified, the next step would be to foster their talent. This means that as much praise, approval and reward must be given to the child who adventures in thought and action as has been given in the past to the child who is tidy, exact and able to reproduce information fed into him.

A further influence of the recognition of creativity may show itself in examination methods, in the use of questions which are open-ended, and in permitting students to use reference books in the examination room, the emphasis being less on memorisation than on the solving of problems.

Diagnostic Tests

The immediate future appears to promise a greater development in

---

[1] E. P. Torrance, *Guiding Creative Talent*, Prentice-Hall, 1962.
[2] J. Guilford, 'The Structure of Intellect', *Psychological Bulletin*, **53**, 1956.

tests of diagnosis than in any other area. We can compare one child with another very well in terms of reading age, or arithmetic age, or spelling age. But what teachers want to know is *why* there are these differences and what form remedial education should take. The problems of why certain children, otherwise intelligent, cannot read or spell, or do simple arithmetic are far from solved and the solutions would appear to depend upon the development of diagnostic tests based upon an accurate analysis of skill-getting processes. We are only just beginning to appreciate the complexity of thought that makes possible the learning of simple skills. It still remains that most learning in school occurs despite the teacher or at least in ways of which the teacher is not fully aware.

Tests of intelligence may also be expected to develop in ways which allow the resulting scores to be presented as profiles or analyses of ability rather than as global assessments, and recognition given to the fact that a child may be more 'intelligent' in one direction than in another. For a discussion of this point see A. Heim, *An Appraisal of Intelligence*, Methuen 1970.

Part Two

Details of Tests

Part Two is mainly concerned with details of actual tests, and in reading it the following points should be borne in mind.

SCOPE OF THE INFORMATION. All that has been attempted is to describe a selection of tests likely to be of interest to teachers and already in use in this country. Those who want a comprehensive list of American and British tests should consult *Tests in Print* (Gryphon Press). The comments on tests in this section are on a simple practical level; and those who want a psychological assessment should consult the latest edition of *The Year Book of Mental Measurement* by O. K. Buros (Gryphon Press).

TIMING OF TESTS. Wherever possible the actual working time for each test has been given. In estimating how long it will take to give a particular test allowance must be made for practice-items, giving instructions, etc. A test composed of many subtests each requiring separate instruction may take at least as long again as the actual working time.

NEW TESTS AND PRICES. While the following pages contain most of the tests in common use in British schools at the time of writing, readers should also consult the latest catalogues supplied by the sources listed on page 154. Prices have not been quoted because of the possibility of frequent changes.

RELIABILITY AND VALIDITY. As the majority of the tests described here have high reliability (in the statistical sense) it has not been thought necessary to quote actual figures. Where a test handbook has been found to contain no reference to the test's reliability or validity this has been stated.

QUALIFICATIONS OF TEST PURCHASERS. Most of the tests reported in the following pages are available to teachers, but some can be obtained only by those holding an appropriate qualification. Each supplier has its own classification which is usually printed in the test catalogue. Where a test is not normally available to teachers, this is indicated.

6

Mental Tests for the Pre-School Child

There has been an increasing amount of evidence during the last few decades that a child's experiences during the first five years of life may have a profound influence on his future development. It is hardly necessary to mention the influence ascribed by Freud[1] to the oral, anal and genital stages of childhood, and how attitudes established during these stages may act as prototypes for subsequent personality patterns. Piaget[2] has described in great detail how the growing baby builds up inside himself a picture of the outside world, and has shown the inevitability of certain stages in intellectual growth. John Bowlby[3] has alerted society to the dangers of depriving young children of maternal care during the first few years of life. Gesell's work in America has been developed and extended in England by Illingworth[4] to evolve methods of diagnosis for detecting abnormalities in babies and young children. There is in fact a great deal now known about the needs and characteristics of the pre-school child's mentality and physical development.

The tests or scales used in the treatment and study of these children may be of immediate interest to teachers in nursery schools and classes, as well as to teachers of young retarded or handicapped children.

[1] *Introductory Lectures on Psycho Analysis*, Allen and Unwin, 1932.
[2] *The Child's Construction of Reality*, Routledge, 1954.
[3] *Child Care and the Growth of Love*, Penguin, 1953.
[4] *Development of Infant and Young Child, Normal and Abnormal*, Livingstone, 1963.

The assessment of ability at this age must, of course, be different in quality from assessments at a later age: in the very early stages it is a matter of measuring physical coordination and simple communication rather than the ability to 'think'.

Gesell Developmental Schedules

4 weeks to 6 years; 1940; untimed; individual; A. Gesell and others; Test Agency, N.F.E.R., Level R.

These schedules consist of statements of what the normal child can do at various age levels in the first six years of life. Some of the tests require the use of special material, e.g. a ring, rattle, formboard, cubes. Four aspects of development are reported: personal-social, language, motor and adaptive behaviour. For each of these aspects a child may be given a 'development quotient'. Despite the fact that some of the items for the older children are the same as those in conventional intelligence tests, a child's total score on this schedule should not be thought of as an I.Q. The procedure to be used is described in *The First Five Years of Life* and in *The Developmental Diagnosis* by Gesell.

Griffiths Mental Development Scale

Birth to 2 years; revised form 1955; individual; untimed; Ruth Griffiths; available only to those who have taken Dr. Griffiths' training course.

To some extent this is a development of the Gesell schedules but covers only two years, is more detailed, and is standardised on British babies. Norms of behaviour are given for five aspects of growth, i.e. locomotor, personal-social, hearing and speech, eye and hand, and performance. For each month of age there are up to three items. A full description of the test, its construction, administration and apparatus is given in the *The Abilities of Babies* by Ruth Griffiths (U.L.P.).

Merrill Palmer Scale of Mental Tests

18 months to 71 months; 1931; 1 hour; Test Agency, N.F.E.R.; Level R.

This is a series of verbal and performance tests requiring the use of special apparatus and standardised on American children.

The Developmental Progress of Infants and Young Children

o to 5 years; 1960; M. D. Sheridan; H.M.S.O.

This booklet includes a chart of development giving descriptive statements of normal attainments under the heading: posture and large movements, vision and fine movements, hearing and speech, social behaviour and play. Details are given for ages 1 month, 3 months, 6 months, 9 months, 12 months, 15 months, 18 months, 2 years, 2½ years, 3 years, 4 years, 5 years.

This is not so much a test as a concise guide for doctors and students of child development. Some of the items on hearing and vision would require the use of materials from Dr Sheridan's vision and hearing tests which are described in the section on Reading Readiness.

The Stanford-Binet Scale of Intelligence

This is suitable for children from the age of two, but its description appears in the next section since it is also suitable for older children.

The Wechsler Pre-School and Primary School Intelligence Scale

4 to 6½ years; 1966; individual; D. Wechsler; Psychological Corporation, New York; Level Q.

Based on the W.I.S.C. Scale (see page 68) this is standardised on six age levels and contains five verbal and five performance subtests to yield verbal, performance, and full scale I.Q.s.

7

Mental Ability Tests which Include Items for Infants

In his introduction to *Intelligence Tests for Children*, Professor C. Valentine stated that every child should have an intelligence test in the nursery school, again in the infant school and again in the junior school. He believed that this would become established practice, and that the teachers would be amply 'rewarded in the greater personal knowledge she gains, not only of the child's intelligence and of some special abilities, but of his temperament'.

Although this was written over twenty years ago, the general testing of infants is no nearer today than it was then. This is not only because teachers dislike labelling children so early in life, but because of the sheer impracticality in terms of personnel and time. Many would say that the educational differences between five-year-olds are so small that measuring their intelligence in unnecessary, and that the organisation of a good infant school does enable the individual needs of each child to be met, and that five-year-olds find the classroom so bewildering and exciting a place that the first year at school is not so much a time for testing as for helping the child to make many adjustments which are demanded of him in his strange new world.

A much better case can be made for giving intelligence tests to older infants, (*a*) because teachers may be wondering why certain children have made so little progress and (*b*) because junior schools may be requesting information about children shortly to come to them. But in fact, intelligence tests are rarely given at this time. When reports of pupils' abilities are passed to the junior school they are often confined to reading or arithmetic ages, and it is on the basis of these that classes or groups are formed. This basis of selection has its dangers.

Recent research[1] has suggested that once in a stream, a child is likely to stay there; and if the stream happens to be the lowest then the consequences for the late developer (or in some cases the younger children) may be unfortunate. There appear to be far fewer transfers from one stream to another than are actually merited, perhaps because teachers adjust themselves to the supposed limitations of their pupils and as time goes on this adjustment of teacher to pupils. and pupils to the teacher's expectations, results in a 'hardening of the categories'. In view of this tendency the assessment of children at this tender age should (a) be seen as temporary and (b) include an assessment of mental ability.

A six-year-old's ability in basic skills may be a poor predictor of his future progress. This is especially so if at the time of the test the child is a 'young' six and, as is often the case, his precise age is not taken into account when this score is recorded. A few months of schooling at this age may produce quite rapid changes.

A better prediction can be obtained by including an assessment of mental ability because (a) an I.Q. contains a built-in allowance for age and (b) what is measured by a mental-ability test is less influenced by privileged opportunities for learning than are reading and number skills.

Although some of the tests described in this section are not designed solely for infants they are included here because their range covers the period five to seven. The tests are in two groups i.e. Level R tests, and those for use by teachers. The Level R group includes only those which are likely to be reported on to teachers and it is hoped that the descriptions given here may help teachers to evaluate more fully the reports they may receive from clinics and psychologists.

Teachers naturally prefer to use group tests because they save time, but when infants are to be tested special difficulties arise.

[1] B. Jackson, *Streaming: An Educational System in Miniature*, Advisory Centre for Education.

Some authorities maintain that infants should not be tested in groups because children so young lack the self-control and the self-motivation which independent working of this kind demands; infants still regard their teachers as something of a mother figure, and few regard copying as unethical. But these strictures should not be taken too seriously. There is little doubt that group-tests can be given successfully to *older* infants as long as certain points are borne in mind:

1. Supervisors should know the children well enough to forestall possible misunderstanding of instructions and to give the children confidence.
2. The size of the group should be no greater than fifteen.
3. If a child's score is very different from what was expected, an individual test should be given, preferably by an expert.
4. The duller children should be tested individually.

Intelligence Tests for Children

$1\frac{1}{2}$ to 15 years; revised 1958; individual; untimed; non-reading; C. W. Valentine; Methuen.

Valentine had no hesitation in recommending his tests for use by the non-specialist. In the preface to *Intelligence Tests for Children*[1] he wrote:

> ... Many teachers with some preliminary training in psychology can learn to apply tests of this kind with sufficient reliability to obtain a much better idea of innate intelligence of their children than can be gained by general impression or even the quality of the work in school, which may be affected by conscientiousness or indifference, by special home help and advantage or disadvantage.

He added that intelligent parents, if they obey instructions strictly and judge impartially, can give his tests and gain valuable information thereby. On this last point, surely it is asking too much to expect impartiality from a parent: the danger of giving the benefit of the doubt, even unconsciously, would seem too great.

Valentine's tests are contained in a small book. A few pieces of simple apparatus are required, which can if necessary be obtained

---

[1] Now out of print but available in some libraries.

from the publishers. Most of the test items have been taken from long-established tests, e.g. mazes from the Porteus Test, reasoning tests from Burt, matching geometric figures from the Stanford Binet, developmental tests from Gesell. The whole battery is an attempt to produce an inexpensive short test of general ability. Nominally for children up to fifteen, the test is offered as most useful for children from two to eight and for dull children within this mental age range. Pupils at the infant level are asked, for instance:

5-year-olds

1. Is it morning or afternoon?
2. Draw a man (drawing should be recognisable).
3. Repeat a twelve-syllable sentence.
4. Define by use a spoon, chair, table, etc.

6-year-olds

1. Repeat five digits.
2. Give the difference between milk and water, man and dog, etc.
3. Repeat sixteen syllables.
4. Complete analogies such as 'a snail goes slowly, a rabbit goes—'?

Valentine stresses the unreliability of test scores by under-fives and advises two testings rather than one; he claims that the tests indicate fairly reliably the present stage of development of the child and his probable capacity for the next few years.

Goodenough-Harris Draw-a-Man Test
5 to 15 years; 1963; individual or group; untimed; Dale Harris; Harrap.

In 1926 Dr F. Goodenough published her Draw-a-Man Test which became widely used as a rough measure of mental ability during the subsequent decades in the United States and Britain. The child's drawing was evaluated by totalling the number of items it contained according to Dr Goodenough's check list.

In 1963 the test was thoroughly revised and restandardised by Dale Harris to produce the Goodenough-Harris Draw-a-Man Test. This differs from the original in that there are more items; the child is now required to draw a man, a woman, and himself; and a quick method of scoring is available using drawings typical of certain ages.

The total score is obtained by averaging the three scores. Harris points out that the test ceases to be discriminating at about the age of 13. The following drawing is by a dull child of 6½ and credited on the Goodenough-Harris scale with a raw score of 9 points because it contains a head, eyes, nose, mouth, chin and forehead, ears, arms, legs and feet.

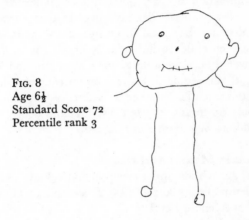

FIG. 8
Age 6½
Standard Score 72
Percentile rank 3

Obviously this test does not measure ability to use language, to classify, reason, handle number-concepts, i.e. most of the factors usually measured by a test of general ability. Nevertheless it has proved to be of value in placing young children roughly in order of intellectual ability and for detecting very dull children. Artistic talent appears to have very little effect on scores, especially at the infant level. Coaching on drawing the human figure is likely to produce an artificial raising of scores.

The fact that according to Harris, between 1926 and 1963 children's ability to draw a man increased significantly, underlines the need, mentioned more than once in these pages, to keep tests up-to-date. *Children's Drawings as Measures of Intellectual Maturity* by Dale Harris not only contains the manual for his test, but also a very thorough account of how the restandardisation was carried out and excellent chapters on the psychological study of children's

63

drawings. The suitability of this test for English children has been strongly criticised.[1]

The Kelvin Measurement of Ability in Infant Classes

5–8 years; 1935; group or individual; timed; 15 minutes; non-reading; C. M. Fleming; Gibson and Co.

This booklet contains pictures of common objects drawn crudely but unambiguously, and has subtests on memory, aesthetic differences, discrimination of size, observation, similarities, counting, completion, classification. Fleming suggests that entrants to the infant school should be tested in groups of 10–15. It would seem wiser to test such children individually or wait until they are six when they would be more able to work in groups and keep to the strict timing that is required. Raw scores for each month of age are convertible to percentiles or standardised scores. As standard scores are given only up to 125, the test discriminates poorly among the brighter children. Standardised in Glasgow.

S.R.A. Primary Mental Abilities

5 to 7 years; 4th edition 1954; group or individual; 3 of 5 subtests timed; total time 60 to 80 minutes; T. G. and C. C. Thurstone; N.F.E.R. Test Agency; Level P.

This 24-page booklet is often used as a source of readiness tests, but by combining the results of the five subtests, verbal-meaning, perception, quantitive, motor and space, an overall score can be obtained. Thurstone recommends the use of a profile and the one illustrated below shows the scores of a typical six-year-old, giving the 'mental age' achieved in each subtest. The manual contains a table for converting mental ages to Total Score Quotients.

The battery was standardised on American children. Although the manual is detailed and clearly written, it contains no evidence of the test's reliability and validity, but a Technical Supplement is available on request.

Coloured Progressive Matrices

$5\frac{1}{2}$ to 11 years; 1958; individual or group; untimed; non-reading; J. C. Raven; Lewis and Co.

[1] See article by M. Sinha, *Brit. J. Ed. Psych.*, June, 1970.

This is attractive and easy to give. On each page of the test book is a large coloured pattern with a piece 'missing', and the child is required to find the missing piece from among several alternatives in the lower half of the page. Older children may take this test as a group but infants should be tested individually,[1] the teacher turning the pages and recording choices. While there is no time limit, the whole test rarely takes more than twenty minutes. A template is available to make marking easy.

Example of an S.R.A. profile for a six-year-old

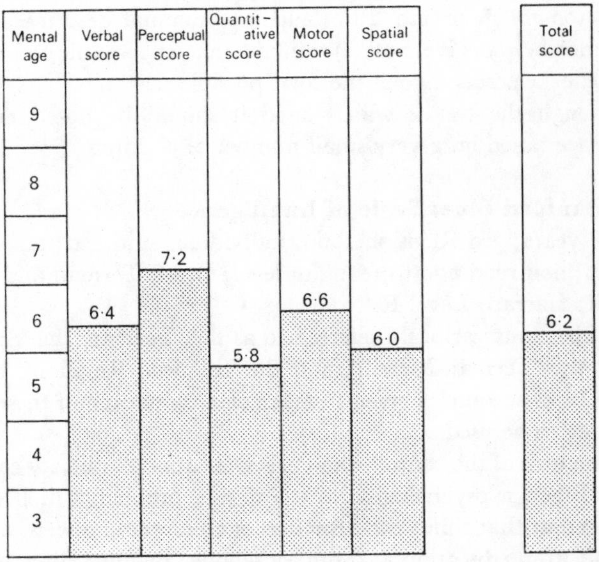

FIG. 9

Raven advises that the test is not one of intelligence but of clear thinking and observation, and that if an estimate of general intelligence is required then the Matrices test should be supplemented by his Crichton Vocabulary test (see page 93). This advice should be taken with caution for while these measures of non-verbal reasoning

[1] For suggested modified instructions for giving Ravens Coloured Progressive Matrices to six- to seven-year-olds, see article by P. S. Freyburg in *Brit. J. Educ. Psych.*, June 1966.

A TEACHER'S GUIDE TO TESTS AND TESTING

and of vocabulary are useful in estimating two aspects of mental
ability they do not cover the wide area that is usually associated
with general intelligence.

The manual provides a table for converting raw scores to percentiles. To convert these percentiles to I.Q.s use may be made of
the table on page 153 of this book.

Because so little needs to be said in giving this test it is obviously
suitable for testing the deaf, those with little English, or those with
speech defects. Some common errors made in giving the Coloured
Progressive Matrices are (a) hurrying the child on too rapidly, (b)
giving too much or too little help (the manual describes exactly
how much help to give) and (c) thinking that a percentile score means
an I.Q. or a percentage of the total possible marks.

Although the test is widely used it should be noted that the
norms are based on a very small number of children.

The Stanford Binet Scale of Intelligence

2 to 18 years; 3rd Revision 1960; individual; untimed; taking 1 to
2 hours; non-reading at the infant level; L. M. Terman and M. A.
Merrill; Harrap; Level R.

As this test is variously referred to as the 'Terman' the 'Stanford
Binet', the 'Terman-Merrill', and the 'Stanford Revision', the following brief account is given to make clear why each of these terms
has come to be used.

At the turn of the century the Paris Education Authority called in
Alfred Binet, a psychologist, to examine a problem which Britain
also faced at that time: the detection of children who were too dull
to profit from education at ordinary schools. By 1908 Binet and his
colleague Theodore Simon had devised a series of graded mental
tasks which could be solved by the normal child at certain ages.
This scale made possible the use of the 'mental-age' device; e.g. a
ten-year-old child who could solve tasks only up to the level normally achieved by seven-year-olds would be credited with a mental
age of seven.

British and American educators recognised the great value of the
Binet-Simon scale and adapted it for use in their own countries. In
1916 Professor Terman of Stanford University produced a version
suitable for American children from three to sixteen years and this

66

became known as the Stanford Binet or the Stanford Revision. The use of the ratio

$$\frac{\text{Mental age}}{\text{Chronological age}} = \text{I.Q.}$$

was introduced in this version. In 1937 the test was completely revised by Professor Terman and Merrill and issued under the title of the New Revised Stanford-Binet Test of Intelligence, more commonly known as the Terman-Merrill Test. This in its turn became out-of-date and was revised in 1960 under the title, 'The Stanford Binet Scale of Intelligence, 3rd Revision'.

Like its predecessor this revision enjoys an international reputation. Since it begins at the two-year-level it is frequently used for testing infants and subnormal children. For each half-year from two to four and-a-half, and for every year from five onwards there are six subtests covering a variety of abilities. The nature of the tests are:

For five-year-olds

Completing the drawing of a man.
Folding a paper triangle.
Defining words.
Copying a square.
Seeing similarities and differences in pictures.
Fitting together two halves of a rectangle.

For six-year-olds

Defining words.
Giving the difference in meaning between certain words.
Detecting what is missing from a picture.
Counting objects.
Solving simple analogies.
Tracing through a maze.

At each age level the nature of the items changes, reflecting the abilities that are believed to develop about that time. Each item successfully answered earns so many months credit, total scores are

67

expressed in years and months of mental age, and these can be converted to I.Q.s. While some questions have a single answer, for others there are several acceptable responses and it is left to the tester to evaluate these according to certain principles. Not only the answers but the child's behaviour during the interview, e.g. over-confidence, nervousness, is noted and may be taken into account when a report on the interview is written. Because of the difficulty of administration and especially of interpretation, it has been suggested that before his results may be accepted as valid, a tester should have tested at least fifty children while under the guidance of an experienced test officer.

Because of its high verbal content it is unsuitable for children whose oral English is poor, e.g. newly arrived immigrants, children with speech or hearing defects, and those coming from verbally impoverished homes. There are special adaptations for the handicapped.[1] Compared with other intelligence tests this one is expensive, owing largely to the cost of the apparatus necessary for testing young children. It is undoubtedly one of the best tests available today.

The Wechsler Intelligence Scale for Children

5 to 15 years; 1949; individual; 30–90 minutes; both timed and untimed items; D. Wechsler; N.F.E.R. Test Agency; Level R.

This is also an American[2] test, popularly referred to as the W.I.S.C. (pronounced 'wisk'). Unlike the Standard-Binet it is unsuitable for children with mental ages below five, contains a considerable number of 'performance' (i.e. practical) tests, and rewards quick thinking. Within the last few years it has come to rival the Stanford-Binet in popularity, one of its outstanding advantages being that it yields for each child three kinds of I.Q.: verbal, performance, and full score.

The verbal subtests concern information, comprehension, similarities, vocabulary, arithmetic, while the performance subtests include jigsaws, picture completions, picture sequences, mazes, codes and block designs. By totalling the scores on the verbal scale separately from those on the performance scale a comparison can

[1] For example, The Williams Intelligence Test for Children with Defective Vision, Birmingham University.
[2] But see the Scottish Standardisation of W.I.S.C., U.L.P. 1967.

be made between these two aspects of intelligence. A full score is obtained by combining verbal and performance scores.

Like the Stanford-Binet it involves the use of a variety of apparatus and is comparatively expensive.

The Porteus Maze Tests
3 to 15 years; 1952; untimed; individual; 10–20 minutes; S. D. Porteus; Harrap; Level R.

Like the original Binet tests, the Porteus Mazes were first designed for testing subnormal children. Unlike most other intelligence tests covering a wide age-range, however, it demands from the child only one kind of activity, namely, tracing through a maze on paper. Porteus points out that intelligent behaviour always involves planning and claims that his test is a measure of 'planfulness', and that whereas the Stanford-Binet measures the kind of intelligence that is required for learning school subjects, his test helps predict how an individual will get along in everyday life.

The mazes are of increasing difficulty, one being allotted to each year of age, from three to twelve, with a further two for ages fourteen and fifteen. The maze reproduced in Figure 10 is intended for six-year-olds.

The examiner asks the child to imagine that the lines are stone walls with spaces between them. The child is asked to draw a line from the rat to the cheese without crossing lines or going up places blocked at the ends, or lifting pencil from paper.

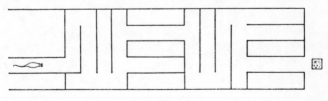

FIG. 10

The test has obvious limitations since it does not require vocabulary, number-sense, classification of words or shapes, etc. and is clearly unsuitable for those with poor manual control. But many psychologists find it useful as a supplementary test, especially where

69

brain-injury, emotional disturbance or anti-social behaviour is suspected. The norms require bringing up to date.

Kohs Block-Design Tests

5 to 19 years; 1919; S. C. Kohs; N.F.E.R. Test Agency; Level R.

This is a performance test, which, while a test in its own right, has often been used as the basis of subtests in other general ability tests such as the W.I.S.C. test. The material consists of sixteen one-inch cubes painted in various colours, and the test consists of building with the blocks each of seventeen coloured patterns which are presented on small cards. Points are lost for excess time taken and an excess number of moves.

8

Mental Ability Tests

For 7-year-olds

For many years the age of seven has been a milestone in the education of British children. It has marked a change from informal to formal methods of teaching more often than we may have wished. Because junior schools request detailed information about their incoming pupils in order to organise classes and groups, and Local Education Authorities often choose this age at which to carry out surveys of attainment, psychologists have produced a number of group tests of mental ability specially for seven-year-olds.

All but a few seven-year-olds are mature enough to be tested in groups, but those few, despite all precautions, may declare themselves by calling out what they think are the answers, or by failing to obey simple instructions. Teachers would be aware of such children and perhaps give them individual tests.

Of the five tests described below, four are called picture tests. While most seven-year-olds can read, many cannot read well enough to follow printed instructions, so the items are in the form of shapes, patterns or pictures, and instructions are given orally. Presenting a test in this way does not lessen to any great extent the possibility of testing the ability to see relationships similar to those found in many verbal tests. For example, an analogy or classification problem can be as easily presented in pictures as in words. The analogy: 'bird is to cage as dog is to . . .' can be presented, with suitable oral instructions about underlining, as shown in Figure 11. A word-classification item such as: 'Which does not belong in the following words, fish, cat, dog, chair, monkey?' may be presented simply as pictures of these things, the instructions being read aloud.

FIG. 11

Picture Test A
7.0 to 8.1 years; 1954; individual or group; 22 minutes; 3 timed subtests on classification, series, analogies, all pictorial; J. Stuart; Ginn for N.F.E.R.

The Deeside Picture Test
6½ to 8½ years; 1957; individual or group; 25½ minutes; 7 timed subtests on directions, classification, sequences, matching, reversals, analogies, series; W. G. Emmett; Harrap.

Moray House Picture Tests 1 and 2
6½ to 8½; 1944; individual or group; 33 minutes; 9 subtests on directions, classification, completion, absurdities, sequences, reversals, 'always has', analogies, series; M. Mellone; U.L.P.

The Deeside and the Moray House Picture Tests are very similar in age range, types of subtests and duration. While the Moray House Test is almost wholly pictorial, the Deeside Test contains a considerable number of items that require a knowledge of letters and numbers. The Moray House Test was standardised largely on an Edinburgh population; the Deeside was standardised in Cheshire.

Carlton Picture Intelligence Test
Forms A and B. 6.3 to 7.0 years; 1962; individual or group; 32 minutes; 8 timed subtests on absurdities, classification, completion, analogies, always has', sequences, 'most like' and series; W. K. Carlton, U.L.P.

The Carlton Test is the only one of his group with two parallel forms. None of the sixty-four items requires a knowledge of letters or numbers. It is the most up-to-date of the whole group, and was standardised on a Glasgow population.

A glance at the contents of these tests shows that their common features are analogies, series, sequences and classification. They do not measure persistence, memory, originality or many other qualities that may be thought to contribute to intelligent behaviour. These group tests give only a rough measure of ability and should not be used as final arbiters. A score of nil (usually equivalent to a standardised score of -70) on these tests does not mean that the child is educationally subnormal, nor does a retardation quotient $\left(\dfrac{\text{Attainment Quotient}}{\text{Intelligence Quotient}} \times 100 \right)$ of 85 mean that he is under-functioning.

9

Non-Reading Mental Ability Tests

For ages between 6 and 14 years

In choosing a so-called 'non-verbal' test one needs to examine the test to see what exactly it measures, for while some are concerned with relationships between shapes or diagrams, others require the child to respond to continual verbal instructions and are not therefore truly non-verbal.

Otis Quick Scoring-Mental Ability Test

Forms A and B, Alpha. 7 to 10 years; 1937; individual or group; timed 20 minutes; 90 items on classifying pictures and designs; A. S. Otis; Harrap.

This is the only American test of the group and has many virtues, e.g. it is short, initial directions enable the child to work right through the test and parallel forms facilitate retesting. On the other hand the test is concerned with only one type of thinking, i.e. classification of pictures or symbols, and was standardised as long ago as 1937.

Culture Free Intelligence Test, Scale 2

Forms A and B. 8 to 13 years; 1949; 14 minutes; R. B. Cattell; Institute of Personality and Ability Testing, Illinois.

This is a non-verbal, non-pictorial test consisting of subtests on series, classification, matrices, and 'conditions'. Cattell claims that it has been used successfully in many different cultures. He suggests that the group being tested are given Form A before given Form B in order to reduce the effects of test sophistication. The standard deviation is 24 and this must be borne in mind when comparing

74

results with those on most British tests which have a standard deviation of 15.

Cattell Intelligence Test Scale 1

Forms A and B. 8 to 11 years; 2nd revised edition of test, 1935; revised edition of manual, 1952; classification of shapes, maze-drawing, obeying instructions, 'always has', picture analogies, reversed similarities, picture completion; R. B. Cattell; Harrap.

Non-Verbal Test BD

8 to 11 years; revised edition 1964–5; 20 minutes; 4 timed subtests on cyphers, similarities, analogies and series; D. A. Pidgeon; Ginn for N.F.E.R.

These two tests are similar in duration and simplicity and in the age range covered. The Cattell test, however, is the older by thirty years and its manual offers no data on reliability or validity. The non-verbal Test BD, since it contains no pictures, is the more 'culture-free'.

Raven's Progressive Matrices, A, B, C, D, E

8 to 14 years, Revised edition 1956; group or individual; untimed; approximately 50 minutes; J. C. Raven; H. K. Lewis.

This book contains two of the sets of problems that appear in the Coloured Progressive Matrices described on page 64, plus three more difficult sets, the whole in black and white drawings. The author suggests that a complementary verbal test, the Mill Hill Vocabulary Scale, should be used with the Matrices to obtain an all-round assessment of intellectual ability. The handbook gives norms for adults as well as for children, but only in the form of percentiles. To change percentiles to standard scores the table on page 152 of this book may be used.

Three tests presented orally

Oral Verbal Intelligence Test

7.6 to 10.11 years; 1973; individual or group; D. Young; U.L.P. This is similar to the author's Non-Reader's Intelligence Test described below but is more difficult. Like the Non-Reader's Intelligence Test it includes norms for less able children who are older than the top limit for normal children; thus children of low ability up to the age of 14.11 may be assessed by this test. A template is issued to facilitate quick marking.

Tomlinson Junior School Test

7 to 11 years; individual or group; 1953 untimed; 90 minutes approx; 2 sets of 8 subtests on obeying instructions, definitions, number series, opposites, reasoning, classification, selection, analogies; T. P. Tomlinson; U.L.P.

Non-Readers Intelligence Test

6.9 to 8.11 years; 1964; individual or group; untimed; approximately 60 minutes; 4 orally presented subtests on riddles, classification, analogies, opposites; D. Young; U.L.P.

These three tests, although requiring little or no reading, demand an understanding of the spoken word. In the Cornwell Test, for example the teacher reads out the words 'slim, fat, plump, rich', and the pupil has to pick the one that is 'most different' and write down its first letter. Slightly modified, this device is used throughout the Non-Reader's Intelligence Tests, for the answer sheet simply contains rows of four letters, and on each row the pupil has to ring the letter which begins the answer-word. Thus the child is asked: 'What is nice to drink and fizzy? Water, tea, milk, pop', and on the row showing the letters w t m p he should ring the letter p.

All three tests are comparatively economical in that a small handbook is the chief expense, and answer sheets are either cheap or easily made. The Non-Readers' Test gives not only its own norms but a table for converting scores to probable Stanford-Binet scores.

The Porteus Maze Test

This test described on page 69, would also be appropriate for this age group.

For ages between 10 and 16 years

Non-Verbal Test DH

10 to 15 years; group or individual; 50 minutes; 1951; 96 items of the Raven's Matrices type; B. Calvert; Ginn for N.F.E.R.

This is very similar to Raven's Matrices test but has more items per page and in the test as a whole. Although the test was made in 1951 new norms were published in 1958. Marking is by stencil and answers are recorded on a single sheet. A shortened version may be given for ages 10½ to 12 years.

Figure Reasoning Test

10 to 16 years; 2nd edition 1962; group or individual; timed 30 minutes; 45 problems; J. C. Daniels: Crosby and Lockwood.

This test is best described as a pocket alternative to the Raven's Matrices, but suited only to the older pupils. The crude printing that marred the 1949 edition was to some extent corrected in the 1962 edition.

Cattell's Culture Fair Intelligence Test, Scale 3

10 to 16 years; 1950–63; R. B. Cattell; Institute of Personality and Ability Testing, Illinois.

This is very similar in design to Cattell's Scale 2 Test, but is intended for older children and 'superior' adults.

Verbal Mental Ability Tests

For ages between 6 and 13 years

Essential Intelligence Test
Forms A and B. 7 to 12 years; Form A 1940. Form B 1949; group
or individual; 45 minutes; F. J. Schonell; Oliver and Boyd.
   A reading age of 8 is needed for this test. There are 100 items,
mostly of the multiple-choice type, including alphabet problems,
synonyms, opposites, analogies, reasoning, series, 'always has',
problems, and classification. Raw scores are converted only to
mental ages.

Maddox Verbal Reasoning Test
9.5 to 10.5 years; 1960; group or individual; 45 minutes; H.
Maddox, Oliver and Boyd.
   This is very similar in format to the Essential Intelligence Test,
containing 100 items in omnibus form and including similarities,
opposites, missing words, 'always has', series problems, 'doesn't
belong'. It is purely verbal and gives good discrimination over this
one year of age.

Cotswold Junior Ability Test. C, D, E
C (1954) and D (1957) 8.4 to 9.9 years; group or individual; 35
minutes; each test consists of 4 timed subtests dealing with sequence,
analogies, series, reasoning, and classification, C. M. Fleming;
Gibson.
   No validity or reliability figures are given.

Cotswold Junior Ability Test F
9.4 to 10.6; 1961; group or individual; 35 minutes; contains 5

subjects which include sequences, classification, analogies, series, reasoning; C. M. Fleming; Gibson.

The Cotswold series are all very similar in format and content and contain slightly more verbal than non-verbal items. Each test was standardised on a complete county age group and the conversion tables give both percentiles and standard scores.

Verbal Test BC

8 to 10½ years; revised edition 1962; group or individual; 30 minutes; 85 items which include analogies, 'always has', classification, synonyms, reasoning, sequences, coding; D. A. Pidgeon; Ginn for N.F.E.R.

This test is not available to schools in Lancashire, Bournemouth and Leicester.

Verbal Test CD

9 to 11½ years; 1959; group or individual; 35 minutes; 85 items including word classification, jumbled sentences, 'always has', series, arithmetic, analogies, alphabet problems, coding, opposites; V. Land; Ginn for N.F.E.R.

This test is not available to schools in Lancashire and Bournemouth.

Verbal Test C

9.4 to 11.0; 1966; group; 35 minutes; 85 mixed items of the type used in Verbal Test CD; Ginn for N.F.E.R.

Verbal Test D

9.6 to 12 years; 1962; group or individual; 84 items including arithmetic, analogies, sequence, 'always has', series, codes, jumbled sentences, opposites, word classification; T. N. Postlewaite; Ginn for N.F.E.R.

The Verbal Tests BC, CD, C, and D, unlike the Cotswold series, contain scarcely any pictorial or diagrammatical material and are deservedly named verbal tests. The manuals appear to be the best in the whole group and respect the teacher's interest in test construction.

In choosing a test from this group it may be noted that the only ones which have parallel forms (for the convenience of retesting) are the Cotswold and the Essential. If purely verbal tests are required then the ones to be considered are the Essential, Maddox and Verbal Tests. Of these the Essential would be least discriminating because of the wide age range it covers; at the same time it does avoid the need to purchase more than one test for the whole of the junior school years.

For clarity of presentation and most recent standardisation the Verbal Tests are clearly superior.

For ages between 10 and 13 years

Although at the time of writing they can still be purchased, many tests for this age range are of the old fashioned eleven plus type, their content, aim and norms, now outmoded. These include the Northumberland Mental Tests, the Thanet School Aptitude Tests, the Northern Test of Educability, and the Southend Test of Intelligence.

A few extracts from their manuals suggest their unsuitability for today, for example, the author of the Thanet Test writes: 'It is not a test of attainment. It is a test of capacity. It is largely independent of the work of the school and, therefore, independent of the work of the teacher.' But in fact the test contains a great deal that can only be learned in school. The manual for the Northern Test of Educability assumes that 'children with mental ratios greater than 123 have been transferred to secondary schools and children with mental ratios less than 70 have been removed to special schools.' The Southend Test of Intelligence is intended 'to grade normal children . . . between 10½ and 13'; but the lowest I.Q. the test can register for 10½ year old is 90.

Some of the authors of these early tests were admirable pioneers, but time has inevitably overtaken this part of their work, which belongs more appropriately to a history of testing than to the present volume.

Cotswold Measurement of Ability—Mental Ability, Series 9 to 12

Series 9 to 11, 10 to 13 years, 1953–58; Series 12, 10.6 to 11.6 years,

1961; group or individual; 30–40 minutes; C. M. Fleming; Gibson.

Each test consists of five timed subtests containing items on word classification, analogies, word and number series, verbal reasoning, coding, arithmetic, alphabet problems, chart interpretation.

The Kingston Test of Intelligence, Forms A and B

10 to 12.11 years; Form A 1952, Form B 1962, Manual 1963; group or individual; 33 minutes; 5 timed subtests on number series, word analogies, shape analogies, 'sometimes true', word series; M. E. Hebron; Harrap.

This test is predominantly concerned with analogies in verbal and diagrammatic form.

Carlton Intelligence Test No. 1

10 to 12 years; group or individual; 45 minutes; 1962; items include word classification, 'always has', jumbled words, analogies of numbers, shape and words, coding, completion, word-ladders, shape classification, opposites, sequences, mixed sentences, true/false, reasoning; H. C. Carlton; U.L.P.

The Carlton Test is the most recently produced of this group. The layout is spacious, the content more varied than that of the Kingston. In choosing a test for children from ten to thirteen it can be seen that the Kingston and the Cotswold Tests both provide parallel tests. The Carlton is the most recently standardised, gives fullest information about its construction and has the most varied content.

Carlton Intelligence Test No. 2

10 to 12 years; 45 minutes; 1965; H. C. Carlton; U.L.P.

The test is mainly verbal but contains some diagrammatic material. Items include opposites, analogies, word-ladders, codes, picture absurdities, etc.

For ages between 10 and 16 years

Otis Quick-Scoring Mental Ability Tests, Beta, Forms A and B

10 to 15 years; 1937; group or individual; 30 minutes; 80 items on word-definitions, analogies, word series, opposites, shape classifi-

cation, arithmetic, proverbs, jumbled sentences, reasoning, alphabet problems, number series, coding; A. Otis; Harrap.

Shorter than most, it is produced in a very professional style, is simple to administer and mark. It has been used for many years in this country despite the fact that its norms are American and even in America has been superseded by other tests.

Verbal and Non-Verbal Test 1

12 to 13.11 years; 1951; group or individual; 45 minutes; 8 timed subtests, 4 of which are verbal (word classification, word analogy, jumbled sentences, reasoning) and 4 non-verbal (shape classification, shape analogy, arithmetic, letter sequence); Ginn for N.F.E.R.

This test gives the opportunity to detect any marked differences between a child's verbal and non-verbal ability. It should be particularly noticed that the practice items are to be given one week before the test proper.

Verbal Test E F

11 to 13½ years; 1960; group or individual; 40 minutes; 90 items on coding, number and letter series, word and number analogies, jumbled sentences, reasoning, synonyms, opposites, word classification, word-linking, opposite-same-rhyme; V. Land; Ginn for N.F.E.R.

This is a continuous test, and the items are presented in mixed sequence rather than in homogeneous groups. It is offered as 'a useful indication of streams where it is not possible to give an attainment test in each subject'.

Verbal Test G H

13.6 to 15.0; 1966; 45 minutes; V. Land; Ginn for N.F.E.R.

A general ability test which includes items such as synonyms, analogies, codes, word classification, jumbled words, verbal reasoning.

A.H. 4 Group Test of General Intelligence

11 to adult; timed; 20 minutes; revised edition 1968; A. W. Heim, N.F.E.R. Test Agency; Level P.

This test is designed for use with a cross-section of the adult population. Part 1 consists of 65 questions with a verbal and numerical bias, Part 2 consists of 65 questions with a diagrammatical bias. Separate norms are provided for each part. Typical scores are given for a variety of subjects, e.g. naval ratings, secondary school pupils, technical college students.

Cattell Intelligence Tests, Scale 11 Forms A and B

11 to 15 years; revised 1950; group or individual; 66 minutes; 6 timed subtests on synonyms, word and shape classification, word-opposites, analogies in words and shapes, sentence completion, inference; R. B. Cattell; Harrap.

The two forms are parallel and can be used for retesting. The standard deviation on this test is 25 points, compared with the usual 15 on British tests. In other words it spreads out the testees more than others tests do, and this may result in children of low I.Q.s generally getting lower I.Q.s and children with high I.Q.s getting higher I.Q.s on this test than on some other tests.

Manchester General Ability Test (Senior) 2

14 to 15 years; 1959; timed 60 minutes; group or individual; 100 items including opposites, synonyms, jumbled words, word classification, analogies. letter series, sequences; S. Wiseman; U.L.P.

These tests were intended to fill a gap in the range of tests then available. The author describes them as parallel but, in fact, they differ in duration, in age level, and in provision of practice items. Senior 1 was standardised on children in 'an English county', Senior 2 on children in the Manchester conurbation. The subtests are alternately verbal and arithmetical.

Tests for higher levels of reasoning

Reasoning Tests for Higher Levels of Intelligence

16 to adult; 1954; 55 minutes; group or individual; C. W. Valentine; Oliver and Boyd.

These are all tests of the verbal reasoning type, designed with particular reference to the selection of candidates for higher education or various branches of the Civil Service. The difficulty of the items range from those passed by most teachers-in-training to those tailed by First Class Honours Graduates. Norms consist of the mean scores of various groups, e.g. undergraduates, teachers-in-training, graduates, boys obtaining Open Scholarships at Oxford or Cambridge. Marking this test is itself a small exercise in reasoning.

Cattell Intelligence Tests, Scale III, Forms A and B

15 to adult; group or individual; revised edition 1952; 66 minutes; R. B. Cattell; Harrap.

Cattell described this test as verbal with perceptual items. It contains six timed subtests on synonyms, classification of words and shapes, word opposites, analogies in words and shapes, completion of sentences and verbal reasoning. Marking is by transparent stencil. The manual contains no evidence of reliability or validity.

Moray House Verbal Reasoning Test (Adult) 1

$13\frac{1}{2}$ to $17\frac{1}{2}$ years; 1961; group or individual; 45 minutes; U.L.P.

This timed test of 100 items includes subtests on verbal classification, reasoning, coding, seriation, analogies, sequences, opposites. It has been used for selecting candidates for teacher-training and is claimed to be useful for grading children of $13\frac{1}{2}$ upwards. A separate table of norms for persons over $17\frac{1}{2}$ is provided. This is a restricted test, see the U.L.P. catalogue.

A.H. 5 Group Test of General Intelligence

13 to 18; timed 40 minutes; A. W. Heim, N.F.E.R. Test Agency; Level R.

This is intended for use with highly intelligent subjects such as university students. It is in two parts, one with 36 verbal or numerical items, and another with 36 diagrammatical items. Norms for several types of subjects are given.

11

Readiness for Reading

While there is little value in giving standardised tests of reading to
five-year-olds, most children are expected to have made a start in
reading by six, and those who have not cause concern. Of these
some will be dull and may not read until they are eight or nine.
But there will be others who have failed to start reading for reasons
other than low intelligence. It should not be assumed that a child
who cannot read lacks all the skills that reading involves. The act of
reading is only the part that shows; it is made possible by the coordination of many minor skills, the lack of any one of which may
impair the child's ability to read. It is essential that these skills, such
as the ability to see differences in shapes, to hear differences in
sound, and to articulate properly, are tested early, so that defects
may be treated and too great demands are not made upon children
who may be incapable of doing better. Because of big classes and an
undermanned school medical service, defects of speech, hearing, and
sight may not be discovered until late in the child's life. The child
may be unaware of his disability and even if aware of it may pre.er
to hide it rather than appear inferior. It is becoming more and more
the case[1] that, because medical inspections are so costly and time-
consuming, recommendations by the teacher based on her day-to-
day observations are being sought to help select those children who
would appear to repay further examination.

If the school medical service fails to test pupils as often as necessary
and a teacher suspects that a child's vision or hearing is below par
what can she do about it?

[1] A 'Method of Screening a School Population for Defective Hearing', *Special
Education*, Vol. LIII, No. 4, 1964.

Tests of hearing and vision for use in the classroom

Let us first establish the importance of hearing for a child learning to read. When a child begins to learn to read he is matching speech with the printed word. But a child learns to speak only by imitating what he is able to hear, and if his hearing is defective then it follows that his learning of both speech and reading will be affected.

A thorough diagnosis of hearing loss can be made only by an audiologist, but there are some simple screening tests which any teacher may use.

The Picture Screening Test of Hearing

From 5 years; untimed; 1960; M. Reed; National Institute for the Deaf.

The test consists of eight cards, each bearing four pictures of common objects and their names. The names on any one card contain the same vowel-sound but different consonants, e.g. cow, house, mouse, owl. The child is shown a card and then asked, from behind to prevent lip-reading, 'Will you show me the house?' 'Will you show me the cow?' etc. Each card is dealt with in this way. Consonants, which are usually more difficult to distinguish than vowels, are the vital clues to what is being said, and any child who has difficulty in hearing certain of these sounds will be detected. Failure on two or more pictures calls for a full examination.

'Getting ready for reading' tests

Books designed as prereaders often contain exercises to test or train aural and visual discriminations. A typical publication of this kind is 'Getting Ready for Reading' (Ginn), the manual for which contains a useful set of hearing tests which any teacher could use in her classroom.

The first of these is the whisper test in which the teacher whispers, from a distance of twenty feet, twenty words selected to include all vowels and consonant sounds. The child is asked to repeat each sound. Failure to repeat two or more of the sounds implies hearing that is inadequate for classroom purposes. In the next test the child is asked to repeat sentences of six simple words, e.g. 'The dog ran after the cat'. This tests retention of what is heard. The third test is concerned with sound-discrimination: from behind the child the tester says certain pairs of sounds such as p-b, th-sh, k-g, and after each pair asks whether the sounds are alike or different.

Stycar Hearing Tests
6 months to 7 years; revised 1968; M. Sheridan; N.F.E.R. Test Agency; Level K.

While the tests mentioned above may be used by the class teacher, there are others, much more exhaustive, which are more suited to the needs of school doctors or peripatetic teachers of the deaf. One is the Stycar Test, consisting of a box of varied materials i.e. sight charts, toys, rattles, bells, word lists, which is recommended for the testing not only of normal children but of defectives and babies. Teachers would need considerable training before using this material.

Auditory Discrimination Test
5 to 8 years; 1958; untimed; J. W. Wepman; N.F.E.R. Test Agency, Level K.

This provides a quick assessment of a child's ability to discriminate between spoken words having similar sounds. It consists of pairs of words spoken by the tester, the subject having to say whether the pairs are the same or different. Typical pairs are cope-coke, shop-shot.

Audiometer tests
The hearing tests most frequently used in schools are those given by audiometrists. The difference between this kind of test and those described above is that the audiometer produces pure tones whereas the tests noted above are concerned with speech tones. Audiometers have their uses, but teachers need to know which particular *speech* sounds the child has difficulty in hearing. Audiograms are sometimes drawn and then left in the pupil's medical records as enigmatical graphs. To be of use they should be explained by a qualified person in terms which the teacher will find of practical use in simple speech training.

Vision tests
Despite the fact that some children are seen screwing their eyes up

or holding books within an inch of their faces they may escape the net of the School Health Service. Perhaps they are absent on the day of the examination, or parents neglect to act on official advice. The most that teachers can do is to continue to report such cases, and where medical help is not forthcoming to use some simple screening device to gain further evidence of defect. There should be a Snellen chart for use by teachers in every school. If a child cannot read it is unlikely that he can name the letters on the Snellen chart. But other methods may be used, e.g. the E chart which bears the letter E printed in various sizes and positions, the child being asked to indicate the direction in which a particular E is facing; pictures or toys may be used instead of letters; or, instead of naming the letters on that chart, he can be asked to match them by reference to a hand-chart.

While sight described as 6/6 is normal, it should not be assumed that sight described as 6/12 is 50 per cent of normal. In these fractions the top figure indicates the distance in feet or metres between the eye and the chart, while the lower figure indicates the particular line, and therefore the size, of print that can be read at that distance. The greater the number indicating size of print, the poorer is the sight. A child with 6/12 vision needs to be at 6 metres from the chart to read what a child with normal vision could read at 12 metres. In other words:

$$\text{Vision} = \frac{\text{Actual distance}}{\text{Normal distance}}$$

Stycar Vision Tests
2 to 7 years; revised 1968; N.F.E.R. Test Agency; Level K.

This is a very detailed test involving the use of a variety of materials and suitable for testing normal children from two to seven years and mentally handicapped children within this range of mental ability.

Reading readiness tests

In discussions about children who have not started to read after a year in the infant school, sooner or later some child will be described as 'not ready'. How can one tell when a child is ready to read?

Some would answer this in terms of the child's natural behaviour, e.g. 'When he spontaneously looks at reading books and asks for the names of letters or words', or 'When he comments on the letter or words around him', Many British psychologists, following the lead of American reports, relate reading readiness to intelligence, quoting a mental age of six and-a-half as necessary before reading can begin. This last suggestion is often useless to infant teachers; in the first place there is little real evidence to support it; in the second place infant teachers are rarely given the mental ages of their pupils.

Instead of using such a vague term as 'mental age' it seems more sensible to ask: 'What specific qualities does a child need before he can start to read?', and having established these, to find a test that will reveal whether a child has them.

Thackray Reading Readiness Profiles
5-year-olds; 1973; group or individual; untimed but about 20 minutes for each of four subtests; D. and L. Thackray; U.L.P.

This is the first British reading readiness test to be published. The subtests are on Vocabulary, in which the child is asked to underline one of four pictures when given its name; Auditory Discrimination, in which the child underlines one of three pictures when given the first sound of its name; Visual Discrimination, in which the child underlines in a row of four the word which matches a given printed word; and General Ability, which is an adaptation of the Draw-a-Man Test. The results are plotted on a chart to make a profile as on the Harrison-Stroud illustration below. At the time of writing, norms for this test were still being established.

Harrison-Stroud Reading Readiness Profiles
6-year-olds; 1956; untimed; 6 subtests on using symbols, visual discrimination; using oral context; auditory discrimination; using oral context and auditory clues; naming letters; M. L. Harrison and J. B. Stroud; N.F.E.R. Test Agency; Level P.

Standardised on American six-year-olds, these are group tests. To indicate answers on the first five the child is required to do only two things, i.e. to draw a line under a picture or word, or to draw a line from one word or picture to another. In the sixth he is asked to name letters.

89

EXAMPLE FROM SUBTEST 1: USING SYMBOLS

This tests the child's understanding that a printed word can stand for a picture. The child is shown pictures of a tree and a book, each with its name beneath. He is the shown a large square in which are the words 'book' and 'tree' at one side, pictures of a book, a table and a tree at the other side, and is asked to draw a line inside the big square from each word to the picture it represents.

EXAMPLE FROM SUBTEST 2: MAKING VISUAL DISCRIMINATIONS

The child is shown rows of words such as

how	how now who hot

and is asked to draw a line under one word in the long box 'to show it is like the word in the little box'.

EXAMPLE FROM SUBTEST 3: USING THE CONTEXT

The context is oral, and items are of the following type. The child is shown a row of pictures in which are illustrated a towel, a cake of soap and a doormat. He is then told: 'After Carl had washed his face and hands his mother told him to wipe them. One picture shows what Carl was told to use to wipe his hands. Draw a line under it'.

EXAMPLE FROM SUBTEST 4: AUDITORY DISCRIMINATION

This test measures the ability to identify initial sounds, e.g. the child is shown pictures of a radio, a turkey and a rabbit and then told: 'Find a radio, a turkey and a rabbit. Draw a line under the radio. The name of one of the other things in the box begins like radio. Draw a line from the radio to the other thing in the box whose name begins like radio.'

EXAMPLE FROM SUBTEST 5: USING THE CONTEXT AND AUDITORY CLUES

Three pictures are shown, one to be selected by using an oral context and auditory clues. For example the child is shown pictures of toes, a kite and a top and given their names. He is then told: 'Tim got a present from his grandfather. What Tim got begins like his name. Draw a line under the picture of the present Tim got.' Each score can be converted to a percentile rank and entered on a graph to produce a profile of reading-readiness skills (see Figure 12). The authors name five types of profile and recommend a special pro-gramme for each type, varying from 'no special instruction' for those scoring a percentile rank of 60 or above in all tests, to a 'year of readiness instruction' for those scoring a percentile rank of 20 or below in four or more tests. A child with results similar to those in Figure 12 would need lessons emphasising the contextual and auditory aspects of reading.

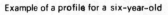

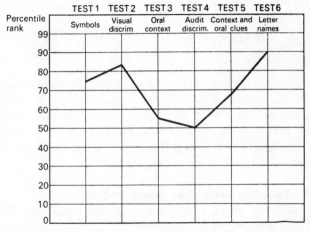

Example of a profile for a six-year-old

Fig. 12

Reading readiness books

Books such as *Reading Readiness* (Nelson), *Getting Ready For Reading* (Ginn) and *Reading For Fun* (Oliver and Boyd) contain bright simple pictures specially designed to start discussion, and devices for teaching the simpler reading skills such as scanning the page from left to right, and identifying the order of sounds in a spoken word.

These books can also be used as tests. For example, in the Ginn booklet there are many rows of pictures which can be used to discover whether a child knows which sound a spoken word starts with, or ends with, or has in the middle. To test whether a child knows how to isolate the initial sound one can present a row of pictures which shows a cap, a cabbage, a teddy-bear and a cat, then ask: 'Which name does not start like all the others?'

To test whether the child can isolate the final sound of a word, a row of pictures could be used showing a tap, a top, a hat and a ship; and for middle sounds a row showing a lamp, jam, a scooter and a cap. It is surprising how many first year infants, and in some cases much older children, need training in listening to words and in the aural analysis of sounds. One of the simplest of tests of this kind, which is given quite spontaneously in many families, is the game of 'I spy something beginning with . . .'.

Vocabulary tests

Reading is based upon talking. A good oral vocabulary is a pre-requisite of reading. Especially in the case of children who are failing to learn to read it is helpful to know whether one of the causes is a poor understanding of words and a sparse oral vocabulary. The following group of tests is designed to test a child's knowledge of spoken words and his use of language.

Reynell Developmental Language Scales

6 months to 6 years; 1968; untimed; individual; J. Reynell; N.F.E.R. Test Agency; Level R.

These scales are intended for the assessment of young children with delayed or deviant language development. There are three scales. Verbal Comprehension A is designed to assess communication ranging from an affective response to a physical or verbal response. Verbal Compreehnsion B is an adaptation of Scale A and is for use with children unable or unwilling to use their hands. The Expressive Language Scale is concerned with spontaneous expression ranging from any vocalisation other than crying to the use of complex sentences.

The material includes toys and pictures. Scoring is in terms of equivalent ages and standard scores; there are separate norms for boys and girls.

The Crichton Vocabulary Scale

$4\frac{1}{2}$ to 11 years; untimed; 1958; J. C. Raven; H. K. Lewis.

This test is intended to be used with Coloured Progressive Matrices which is described on page 64. The Scale consists of a list of words increasing in difficulty, which have to be defined by the child. The child may either read or be told the words. Scores are in percentiles.

Mill Hill Vocabulary Scale

$4\frac{1}{2}$ to adult; 1943; untimed; individual; 10 to 20 minutes; J. C. Raven; H. K. Lewis.

The scale consists of two parallel sets of forty-four words and is intended as complementary to Raven's Progressive Matrices (A, B, C, D, E) but may be used separately. The child simply gives definitions of the words, either orally or in writing. The report forms differ slightly in content according to whether the child is a junior, senior or a non-reader. Norms are given in percentiles.

An English Language Scale

4 to 9 years; untimed; individual; 1944; F. J. Watts; Harrap.

This test is published in *The Language and Mental Development of Children*. The child is asked to describe a graded series of pictures whose content is such that as the child progresses from one to another he needs to use sentences of increasing complexity. Starting at the basic age of four, there are four pictures for each year of age, and three months are added to the score for every picture adequately described. Examples are as follows:

Age level	What the picture shows	Acceptable description
4 years	A person performing an action	A girl skipping
5 years	Relationship between two persons	A boy shaking hands with another boy
6 years	Relationship between three persons or objects	A lady on a horse which is jumping over a gate

There is no evidence of reliability or validity.

93

English Picture Vocabulary Tests

3 to 18+ years; 1962–8; group or individual; untimed; M. A. Brimer and L. M. Dunn; Educational Evaluation Enterprises.

These tests are an English development of the original Peabody Picture Vocabulary Test. They are valid tests of listening vocabulary for normal children, yet are particularly useful for testing handicapped children.

The material for Test 1 and 2 is in the form of non-expendable books of pictures of common objects. Test 2 Group Form and Test 3 are each produced as an expendable double sheet of smaller pictures. In each item the child has to identify from a group of four pictures one which is named by the tester.

The handbook gives considerable information about the construction of the test and provides conversion tables to produce standard scores and percentiles.

Details of the three tests are: Pre-School Version, 3 to 4.11 years, 1969, individual; Test 1, 5 to 8.11 years, 1962, individual; Test 2, 7 to 11.11 years, 1962, individual; Test 2, Group Form, 7 to 11.11 years, 1970, group; Test 3, 11 to 18+ years, 1970, group.

Articulation

If a defect of speech prevents the child from repeating accurately the letter-sounds being taught, this is likely to slow down his learning to read. Many infants, of course, have not mastered all the sounds for speech when they start school, but most do accomplish this by the time they are seven. It is useful for a teacher to know exactly which sounds a child cannot make, so that, perhaps with the cooperation of the local speech therapist, remedial exercises can be given.

To discover a child's precise speech difficulties one might use the Picture Screening Test of Hearing described above, supplemented by other pictures. By asking the child to name pictures whose names include all the speech sounds one may discover those sounds which cause difficulty. At the infant stage one can expect difficulty over the sounds s, th, r, l, and y.

A child may be able to say a particular sound when it occurs at the start of a word but not when it occurs at the end or in the middle of a word, e.g. the 't' in tap may be said correctly but 'little' may be pronounced 'lickle'. A child's particular weaknesses could be recorded, noting the sounds and the position in which they cause difficulty.

During the infant years, when the child is still in the process of mastering speech, help in speech should be more a matter of judicious guidance by the teacher rather than the calling in of a speech therapist.

The Edinburgh Articulation Test

3 to 6 years; 1971; individual; T. T. S. Ingram; Churchill Livingstone.

Though standardised on 3- to 6-year-olds this test is useful diagnostically on older children who are slow or deviant in speech development. It consists of a naming game using 41 cards on which are depicted 68 items, the names containing consonants or clusters of consonants (vowels are not tested) in various positions. Scores can be given either as articulation ages or articulation quotients.

Reading readiness for older children

Although this chapter has been written with infants in mind, much of it has relevance to older children who have failed to learn to read. There still occur instances of junior and even senior children suffering from visual or auditory defects which have gone for years undetected. For such children some of the tests in this chapter should be considered, in addition to the diagnostic tests referred to later.

12

Testing Reading

How reading tests differ from each other

If a child's score on reading test X is different from his score on reading test Y, how can we tell which, if either, is correct? Before this can be answered it has to be recognised that reading tests do not all measure the same thing. This variety is useful, as long as the nature and limitations of each tests is appreciated. The following brief description of a few tests in common use today shows in how many ways they differ from each other.

Name of test	*Age-range*	*Type of test*
Burt Re-arranged Word Reading Test. 1938.	4 to 14	Graded words, read aloud; individual.
Southgate Group Reading Test 1. 1962	6 to 7½	Single words spoken by tester to be chosen from 5 alternatives and underlined; group.
Holborn Reading Scale 1948	5½ to 11	Graded sentences read aloud.
Neale Analysis of Reading Ability. 1958	6 to 13	Illustrated short stories read aloud and questions to be answered; individual.
Southgate Group Reading Test 2. 1962	7 to 9	Incomplete sentences read silently, the final words to be chosen from alternatives and underlined; group.

Even from this short list it can be seen that reading tests differ in their content, age range, method of administration, type of response required and date of standardisation. No single test will give a full picture of a child's reading ability, and the best we can do is to choose the one which best suits the occasion and be aware of the test's limitations.

Choosing a test

In choosing a test it is necessary to know roughly the reading age and actual age of the child to be tested, for the age range of tests varies from one year in the case of the Lambert seven plus test, to fifteen years in the case of the Vernon Graded Word Test. A test with a wide age range is useful in situations where a wide variety of reading ages may be encountered, and where a quick initial estimate is needed; but where a detailed assessment is required then the nearer the scope of the test is to the child's reading ability the better.

To obtain a true comparison between a child's ability and current norms it is important to use a test that has been recently standardised. This is not to say that one cannot measure progress, as distinct from obtaining a reading age, by using a fairly old test as long as its material is well graded.

Silent reading tests, as well as being obviously suitable for giving to whole groups at a time, are particularly useful for children with speech defects or who are embarrassed by reading aloud. But a score on a silent reading test is often based on answering questions on comprehension, and this needs to be remembered when comparing a child's score on this kind of test with those made on a 'mechanical' reading test.

Group tests are appropriate when testing has to be done speedily and only a rough assessment is necessary. But to discover a child's attitude towards reading and his precise ability, an individual test needs to be used, preferably one designed to give diagnostic information as well as a reading age.

To be tested fairly a child should be given a test that has been standardised on children who have had learning opportunities similar to his own. If a child has been taught on predominantly phonic methods then the test chosen should have a phonic rather than a look-and-say bias. The striking difference between tests in this respect may be seen by comparing the first few words of the Schonell Graded Word Reading Test with those of the Standard Reading Test.

Schonell's Graded Word Reading Test (5-year-level)
Tree little milk egg book school sit frog playing bun

Standard Reading Test (5-year-level)
Has a cat legs? Has a cup a lid? Is an egg red? Can a dog run?

Some of the words in the first row, e.g. tree, school, little, are not the kind which a child just beginning to learn to read can build up by putting together letter-sounds. They are words which were probably learned by the look-and-say method from the books used in the particular schools where Schonell standardised his test. But all the words in the second test obviously can be put together by a child who has learned to blend simple three-letter words. Whether a child could do better on one or the other of these two tests at this level would depend to some extent upon the kind of teaching he had received and the particular words he had met.

Choice of test is sometimes influenced by cost. Two main factors affect cost, i.e. purchase price and testing time. Individual tests usually require the purchase of only one test card or test booklet, because the child reads aloud and does not have to mark or write anything. Group tests on the other hand usually require the child to indicate his responses on an answer sheet that may not be reusable. So if many children have to be tested, an individual test will be cheaper than a group test in terms of purchase price, but dearer in terms of the tester's time.

For example, a particular group reading test available at the time of writing costs 25p for the manual and 3p for each test paper, and takes half-an-hour to give; whereas a certain individual graded-word test costs 20p for the manual and 2p for the test card, and at three minutes per child would require ninety minutes to test thirty children. So as far as the cost is concerned the choice is between £1.15 and half-an-hour of the teacher's time, and 22p and ninety minutes of the teacher's time.

It should be remembered in giving the group test to greater numbers of children more test booklets would have to be bought, whereas the test card or booklet for the individual test will serve for many hundreds of children. The best compromise would seem to be to find a satisfactory group test which does not require an expensive answer paper. As we shall see, some group tests leave the preparation of answer sheets to the teacher.

Recording results

As recorded test scores may need to be read by persons other than the tester, it is important that the result is put down fully and clearly. An entry such as 'Reading age, 7.4', may mean much more to the person who writes it than to a stranger. Even when improved to 'Reading age (Neale Test), 7.4' it may not be satisfactory, for this author may have produced many tests or several forms of one test. The Neale Test happens to be an excellent example of the possible ambiguities that may arise in this context for it has three Forms, A, B, C, and three kinds of score, i.e. accuracy, rate, and comprehension. Thus an adequate record of a score on this test should include both Form and aspect of reading tested, e.g. 'Reading age' (Neale test, Form A, Accuracy) 7.4 years'. In all cases, of course, the date of testing would be entered, as well as the tester's name.

Giving the test

We have already discussed the need to maintain standard condition when giving objective tests. One way of lessening variations in the way tests are given is to allow only one person to do or at least supervise, the testing. Not only does this lessen variations due to personal quirks but it enables one person to become skilful in test administration. It may be argued that it is easier for a class teacher to establish the necessary rapport with her own pupils than it is for any other member of the staff. But the practice of teachers giving objective tests to their own pupils has its dangers. Some teachers see low test results as a criticism of their own industry and skill, and this may produce a subconscious urge to obtain good scores, resulting in lenient marking.

Teachers who spend a great amount of time teaching the early stages of reading and for whom phrases such as 'Now what does it start with?' have become second nature, often cannot restrain themselves from helping children during reading tests.

The responses of the impartial and the 'helpful' teacher are typified below, in testing a child on the passage 'A little kitten came to my house'.

Child's reading	Impartial tester	'Helpful' tester
A (pause)	Yes. What comes next?	Now what does it start with? Build it up. You have seen this word before in your little red reader. Remember?
little	Good.	That's right, always build it up.
kit	(No comment)	Now don't forget to look how the word ends.
cam to	(No comment)	Cam? Look at the 'e' on the end. What does that mean you have to do?
my horse	Thank you. A good try.	Is it really horse? How do you say 'ou'? Read it all now—'A little kitten came to my . . . what?

Of course the tester should not maintain an icy silence. The object is to discover what the child is capable of at his best, and this will not be revealed if the child is tense and afraid. There needs to be a friendly relaxed atmosphere. The child needs to be told why the test is being given, i.e. to help the teacher choose the kind of reading which will best suit the child. It is usually advisable to warn the child that there may be many words he cannot read and that these are for older children. To maintain a friendly attitude and relaxed atmosphere is reasonably easy when dealing with only one child, but in giving a group test the very fact that everyone is doing the same thing may engender a spirit of competition which will not be to the advantage of everyone, and needs to be played down. In giving individual tests to a larger number of children the tester should be on guard again his own fatigue. Adopting a friendly attitude to one child after another in rapid succession may become so wearing that the testing becomes obviously a tiring bore; testing should be stopped when this situation appears imminent.

Reading the instructions

It is not uncommon to find reading tests being given without the tester having read the author's instructions. This often happens where the instructions are not bound in the same cover as the test, resulting in the instructions being passed on by word of mouth, and suffering considerable distortion on the way. As we have seen, tests differ so much in their construction and standardisation that it is imperative that the instructions should be read by whoever gives the test, paying particular attention to timing, assessment of errors, when to stop testing, method of recording and the amount of help the child is allowed to receive. The need for instructions to be adhered to rigidly is another justification for having one member of staff responsible for seeing that objective tests are given properly.

Individual tests of reading—graded words

Burt Rearranged Word Reading Test
4 to 15 years; 1938; a card of 110 graded words; untimed; C. Burt U.L.P.

In 1921 Burt published his Graded Vocabulary Test. Seventeen years later P. E. Vernon restandardised this for Scottish children, finding in the process that each word had to be moved up or down an average of five places. This version is now widely used under the title of the Burt Rearranged Word Reading Test. It is unreliable at the extremes, since the first and last ten words have been chosen arbitrarily to represent the ages stated. Burt's advice to teachers of infants and poor readers is worth noting:

> The reading-ages of four and five pretend to little more than conventional significance since at this period a child may not have received even his first lesson in reading. With pupils of this age

or stage it will be wiser to declare . . . that they can read so many two-or-three-letter words.

Burt did in fact provide a test[1] of two- and three-letter words with norms for speed and accuracy for this purpose.

It will be seen that the Rearranged Word Reading Test is now older than was the original when Vernon revised it. However, new norms were established for Edinburgh children in 1954, and this sheet can be obtained from the publisher.

The Graded Word Reading Test

5 to 21 years; 1938; a card of 130 words; untimed; P. E. Vernon; U.L.P.

When Vernon revised Burt's Graded Vocabulary Test he also devised a graded word test for Scottish pupils. Those who wish to use this for infants should note that Vernon wrote:

> It should not be assumed that the first nine words really correspond to the average reading ability of children aged 5 to 5.9 . . . The term 'average reading ability' has no practical meaning until about $6\frac{1}{2}$ years. It seemed advisable to include these fourteen words both as to provide an easy introduction to the test for young children and to enable the tester to score subnormal ability in 6–7 year olds.

Similarly for words above the 15-year-old level Vernon warns:

> We would claim then that although the last 30 words of the scale possess no accurate empirical basis of standardisation yet they will provide testers with a rough gauge of superior reading ability among older children, adolescents, and adults. . . .

The instructions for giving both of the above tests are in *The Standardisation of a Graded Word Reading Test* by P. E. Vernon (U.L.P.)

Graded Word Reading Test, R.1 (also called Graded Reading Vocabulary Test)

5 to 15 years; 1945; a card of 100 graded words; untimed; individual; F. Schonell, Oliver and Boyd.

[1] 'Test 3 Discontinuous Ungraded Test', *Mental and Scholastic Tests*, Staples.

Again it should be noted that the first ten words have not been standardised on five-year-olds. Of the three graded-word tests noted so far, Schonell's test is the most appropriate for English pupils. Instructions for this test are in *Reading and Spelling Tests* (Oliver and Boyd).

RELATIONSHIP BETWEEN BURT AND SCHONELL TESTS. There often arises a need to compare scores on the Burt Graded Word Test with those on the Schonell Graded Word Test, e.g. where children entering a junior or secondary school come from schools which have used both types of tests. A table which allows the conversion of scores on one of these tests to probable scores on the other is in the pamphlet *Reading Ability* (H.M.S.O., 1950).

Marino Graded Word Reading Scale

5 to 19 years; 1967; card of 130 words; untimed; J. Sullivan, Longman, Browne & Nolan, Dublin.

This is similar in appearance and structure to the Burt Rearranged Word Reading Test but has been constructed for use in Ireland. The words have been standardised on a widely representative sample of Irish children.

Individual tests of reading—sentences

Holborn Reading Scale

6½ to 11 years; 1948; 33 graded sentences; untimed; A. F. Watts; Harrap.

The sentences are graded both for comprehension and word recognition. Ideally this would allow a comparison of the two measures but there are norms only for mechanical reading. There is a list of comprehension questions but in the absence of norms and adequate directions these are of limited use.

Standard Test of Reading Skill

5 to 9 years; 1958; 36 graded sentences; untimed; J. C. Daniels and H. Diack; Chatto and Windus.

This is one of a battery of tests contained in *The Standard Reading Tests*. Each sentence is a question, e.g. 'Is it wet?' Marks are not given for correct answers; the question form is used simply to stimulate interest. The grading of questions is based not only upon statistical data but upon phonic difficulty. Scores are given as reading ages and as 'standards'. Standard One indicates an understanding that letters stand for sounds and that letter-order is important; Standard Two represents a mastery of consonantal blends; and so on up to Standard Six. No reliability or validity is offered. This test is intended to be used in conjunction with various diagnostic tests contained in the same volume, and will be described in the section on Diagnostic Tests Related to Reading.

Individual tests of reading—continuous prose

Simple Prose Reading Test (R.2)
6 to 9½ years; 1945; a single page of continuous prose; F. Schonell; Oliver and Boyd.

The pupil reads aloud a 168-word passage called 'My Dog' and is then asked 15 questions. The average score for each half-year of age from 6 to 9½ is given for accuracy, speed and comprehension. Answers to questions are to be given orally. No reliability or validity is offered. Instructions are published in *Reading and Spelling Tests*.

Neale Analysis of Reading Ability
6 to 12 years; 1958; 3 parallel forms; untimed; scored for speed, accuracy, comprehension; M. D. Neale; Macmillan.

In her handbook the author points out that while the graded-word reading scales of Burt, Ballard, Schonell and Vernon were useful measures of word pronunciation, their usefulness for diagnostic purposes was limited, and the prose tests of Burt and Schonell were neither up to date nor had alternative forms for retesting. The Analysis of Reading Ability was offered as retaining the best features of these tests while providing a new format to make the material more stimulating for the poor reader.

Each of the three parallel forms contains six short stories. The first is only four sentences long and in large print, while later stories are longer and in smaller print. When the book is open the left-hand page shows a full-page illustration to arouse interest and focus attention upon the story opposite. Questions are asked after each short story. Supplementary tests are provided to test names and

104

sounds of letters, auditory discrimination and blending of syllables. The record-sheet is perhaps unnecessarily long but facilitates the detection and recording of specific errors and attitudes. This test is clearly superior to the prose tests noted above, both in grading and appearance and in that it offers reasonable evidence of its reliability and validity.

Group tests of reading

Word Recognition Test
5 to 8½ years; 1964; group or individual; untimed; C. Carver; U.L.P.

The test consists of fifty words, and the child is asked to underline in each row the word dictated by the teacher. The words include those of simple structure, e.g. pen, man; combined vowels, e.g. ou aw; double consonant beginnings, e.g. pl gr; endings such as ight. The test gives not only a reading age (or power as Carver prefers to call it) but also, by virtue of the kind of wrong choices the child may make, a picture of the child's specific difficulties. The test has been standardised on over a thousand seven-year-olds in the Manchester area.

Southgate Group Reading Tests: Test 1, Word Selection
Parallel Forms A, B, C,; 6 to 7½ years; 1959; untimed; V. Southgate; U.L.P.

This test is intended for the speedy assessment of children in the first stage of learning to read. Most of the graded word tests in common use during the past twenty or thirty years are unsuitable for testing infants, and it was with the intention of providing a group test for these children that this one was devised. Instead of the usual rows of words that become visibly more difficult down the page, this test is in an attractive illustrated booklet. The child is asked to underline, from sets of five, one word dictated by the teacher.

Southgate Group Reading Tests: Test 2, Sentence Completion
Parallel Forms A and B; 7 to 8.11 years; 1962; timed 15 minutes; V. Southgate; U.L.P.

This test is consecutive to Test 1 but with a slight overlap. It consists of forty-two sentences; at the end of each sentence are five underlined words one of which the child has to ring to show his choice of the best ending. As the instructions for both forms are the same, the two forms can be distributed to alternate children to reduce the danger of copying. Norms are given in reading age and percentiles. It would be useful for bright older infants and the poorer readers in the junior and secondary schools.

Group Reading Assessment

7.8 to 9.0 years; 1964; 3 timed subtests totalling 30 minutes; F. Spooncer; U.L.P.

This test combines both word-recognition and sentence-reading techniques. Part 1 items are of the type: Draw a line under the word 'pit' (child selects from the row 'pet, tip, pit, bit, top'). Part 2 items are of the sentence-completion type, e.g 'A dog will (well, fly, ride, jump)'. Part 3 items are rows of words such as 'too two, low, ton, to, chew' the child having to underline a word which sounds the same as the first word of the row.

Spooncer found that the median reading ages for ten-to-eleven-year-old children taking Schonell's Graded Word Recognition Test was at least nine months higher than the average actual age. This discrepancy between 1964 standards and those established many years previously led Spooncer to produce two conversion tables in his manual, one being the true scores based on his own test, and the other based on what the children would have obtained on the out-of-date Schonell test; the latter table being provided because such ages form the basis of publishers' suggestions as to the suitability of particular books or reading schemes.

Reading Test AD

7.6 to 11.1 years; 1956; 35 graded sentences; timed 15 minutes; A. F. Watts, Ginn for N.F.E.R.

In each sentence the child is required to underline the correct final word from five alternatives. The range may be indicated by the first and last items:

1. Come with me to the shops to buy some (fire, water, stone, sweets, motors).

35. The political dangers of monopoly seems to have been much (exasperated, excised, exaggerated, expropriated, expostulated).

The presentation is extremely clear and spacious, and the marking quick and simple.

Prawf Darllen Brawddegau
8.0 to 10.11 years; 1959; 15 minutes; 35 graded sentences; G. J. Evans; Ginn for N.F.E.R.

This test is very similar to the Sentence Reading Test 1 but is written in Welsh and was standardised on Welsh children.

GAP Reading Comprehension Test
Reading-ages 7.5 to 12.6 years; 1970; timed 15 minutes; J. McCleod and D. Unwin; Heinemann Educational Books.

There are two parallel forms, R and B, each consisting of a four-page leaflet containing eight short passages in which omitted words have to be written in by the pupil. The test was originally standardised in Australia, but the scoring tables have been re-calculated after trials in the U.K.

Group Reading Test
6.6 to 12.11 years; 1968; timed 13 minutes; two parallel forms; D. Young; U.L.P.

This test is on a single sheet, one side containing 15 word-picture matching items and the other side 30 sentence-completion items. It thus incorporates the methods used in Southgate 1 and 2. This test will not discriminate well among above-average children at the higher end of the stated age-range, but does discriminate well across the whole range of ability for children from 6½ to 9 and gives norms for the duller pupils over 10 years of age. A table is supplied giving the scores on other tests that are equivalent to the scores on the Young test. Marking is facilitated by transparent stencil.

Silent Reading Test A
6.9 to 12.8 years; 1945; 18 unrelated paragraphs; timed 9 minutes; F. J. Schonell; Oliver and Boyd.

This is intended for pupils having difficulty in word recognition. One question per paragraph has to be answered on a sheet prepared by the teacher. Separate reading-age norms at half-yearly intervals are provided in *Reading and Spelling Tests*. No reliability or validity evidence is offered.

Silent Reading Test B

(R4) 6.7 to 13.7 years; 1945; 20 unrelated paragraphs; timed 15 minutes; F. J. Schonell; Oliver and Boyd.

As with Silent Reading Test A, the teacher must provide an answer sheet. In each paragraph two or three words are omitted, and the pupils have to select the missing word from a row of five alternatives. It is intended for 'older pupils having little difficulty with word recognition, to gauge their power of comprehension', and is more difficult that Test A. Separate reading-age norms for boys and girls are provided in *Reading and Spelling Tests*. No validity or reliability evidence is offered.

Reading Test A

7 to 8.6 years; 1970; untimed but about 30 minutes; Ginn.

This test is of the sentence-completion type and differs from the Reading Test AD in that the omitted word is rarely at the end of the sentence.

Reading Test B D

7 to 11.4 years; 1969; 20 minutes; Ginn.

A sentence-completion test of 44 items. Standard error of measurement is explained and the S.E.m for each age is given.

The Edinburgh Reading Tests

Stage 2, 8.6 to 10.6 years; Stage 3, 10.0 to 12.6 years; timed; 1972 and 1973 respectively; Godfrey Thomson Unit and Moray House College of Education; U.L.P.

These are tests of higher-order skills. Each stage has three parts, i.e. a practice test, Part 1, and Part 2. In Stage 2, Part 1 has subtests on Vocabulary, Comprehension of Sequences, and Retention of Significant Details; Part 2 has subtests on Use of Context, Reading Rate, Comprehension of Essential Ideas. In Stage 3, Part 1 has subtests on Reading For Facts, Comprehension of Sequences, Retention of Main Ideas; Part 2 has subtests on Comprehension of Points of View, and Vocabulary.

Each stage requires at least 105 minutes to administer, not counting two intervals prescribed to last at least 75 minutes in total. Separate norms are given for Scotland and for England and Wales.

Graded Test of Reading Experience
6 to 14 years; 1959; untimed; J. C. Daniels and H. Diack; Chatto and Windus.

This consists of fifty items of the sentence-completion type. The material is in *Standard Reading Tests* by the same authors and if given as a group test must be duplicated by the user. No evidence of reliability or validity is offered.

Reading Comprehension DE
10 to 12 years; 1967; untimed; E. L. Barnard; Ginn for N.F.E.R.

This test is designed to measure a child's ability to recognise the meaning of a whole passage, extract particular facts, and use imaginatively the facts given. Scores on these different aspects of understanding can be used diagnostically.

Reading Tests E H, 1 to 3
11 to 15 years; 1966; S. M. Bate; Ginn for N.F.E.R.

Test 1 is on vocabulary, average working time 15–20 minutes.

Test 2 is on comprehension, average working time 40–45 minutes.

Test 3 is a continuous prose (speed) test for 11- and 12-year-olds (time limit 7 minutes) and 13–14-year-olds (time limit 4½ minutes).

The Reading Comprehension Test for Personnel Selection
15+; 1972; group or individual; 15 minutes; L. R. C. Haward; U.L.P.

This test has been designed for helping in the selection of applicants for courses of training that rely extensively upon textbooks, its main function being to indicate special training or teaching needs.

Diagnostic tests related to reading

Slowness in reading is sometimes due to a specific difficulty which, if identified, may be treated and cured. The child may always stumble over the same word, or reverse words, or confuse letters such as b and d, h and n, p and q. Teachers spot some of these difficulties in the day-to-day work of the classroom, but this level of observation falls short of what can be achieved by using a diagnostic test. Before listing the diagnostic reading tests that are available here is an example of the information that can be extracted from such a test. The following are a few of the errors made by J. H., a boy with a reading age of six-and-a-half, when doing the Word Recognition Test.

Printed words	Dictated word	Word underlined
in chin ship shin thin	chin	shin
uos was sow aws wor saw	was	aws
jest just jit jast jut jast	just	jast
vu to ox of uv for	of	for
aws sau saw for was sam	saw	for
loud dark doul lead lood	loud	lood
nurn been bown dig burn	burn	bown
dus sub pus bus usb bas	bus	dus

Here one can see a confusion between ch and sh, a tendency to reversal, difficulty with b and d, and mistakes over vowel sounds.

Get Reading Right

For pupils with reading-ages below 9; untimed; 1971; S. Jackson; Gibson.

This consists of a set of diagnostic tests, a handbook of remedial exercises, and a Phonic Skills Record Card. The tests are on separate sheets, each dealing with a specific reading-skill, e.g. letter-sounds, 2- and 3-letter words, consonant blends, vowel digraphs, word-endings, multi-syllable words etc. The handbook contains numerous remedial exercises and suggestion directly related to errors revealed by the Phonic Skills tests. The Record Card enables the teacher to keep a cumulative record of each pupil's progress in phonic skills. This material therefore provides diagnosis, remediation, and recording in one unified scheme.

For the benefit of teachers of infants and subnormal pupils the test of letter-sounds and letter-names is designed to be given as a group-test as well as to individual pupils.

Domain Phonic Test and Workshop
Individual; 1972; J. McLeod and J. Atkinson; Oliver and Boyd.

This scheme is similar to Get Reading Right but has a narrower range and a more complicated marking system. The test consists of four cards for testing phonic knowledge, a record booklet for each child which also contains a test of auditory discrimination, and there are a number of separate sheets on which are printed exercises to cater for specific errors.

Test of Analysis and Synthesis of Words Containing Common Phonic Units
(R5) 1945; F. J. Schonell; Oliver and Boyd.

This is a single sheet of ninety graded words chosen to represent most of the common phonic combinations and families. Its purpose is to estimate the reader's power to analyse words into their phonic constituents and recombine them into word-wholes.

Test of Directional Attack on Words
(R6) 1945; F. J. Schonell; Oliver and Boyd.

This is a page of forty-eight words chosen to reveal any tendency to reverse or part-reverse. Typical words are pot, pit, of, dog.

Visual Word Discrimination Test
(R7) 1945; F. J. Schonell; Oliver and Boyd.

This consists of twenty-five rows of words designed to test visual perception of words. The correctly spelt word is briefly shown on a small card then the pupil is asked to find the same word in a row containing the correctly spelt word among five wrongly spelt versions.

The above tests, R5, R6, R7, are in *Diagnostic and Attainment Tests*.

The Standard Reading Tests, 2 to 9
1958; untimed; J. C. Daniels and H. Diack; Chatto and Windus.

This is a battery of diagnostic tests to be used independently or in conjunction with the Standard Test of Reading Skill which is contained in the same book. The tests include, copying abstract figures, copying a sentence, visual discrimination and orientation, letter recognition, aural discrimination, diagnostic word recognition, oral word recognition, picture word recognition.

Durrell Analysis of Reading Difficulty

6–12 years; 1955; individual; 30 to 60 minutes; D. Durrell; N.F.E.R. Test Agency.

This is an American battery of diagnostic tests for the intensive analysis of reading problems. It includes tests of oral and silent reading, listening comprehension, word recognition, word analysis, phonics, faulty pronounciation, spelling and handwriting. Some of the tests involve the use of a simple tachistoscope (a neat cardboard device for exposing each word for only a fraction of a second). There are supplementary tests which include the naming and matching of letters, identifying sounds, visual memory of words, hearing sounds in words, a knowledge of single and double consonant sounds.

This test has a much wider scope than any of the British tests. The norms of achievement are based on American grade-levels. Selected sections could be used for British children and would give valuable information. It is a test for the reading specialist rather than the average class teacher.

Illinois Test of Psycholinguistic Abilities Second Edition

2 to 10 years; 1968; 45 to 60 minutes; individual; S. A. Kirk, J. M. McCarthy, W. D. Kirk; N.F.E.R. Test Agency. Level P.

This test, which is designed to diagnose difficulties in the understanding and use of language in young children, is a revised edition of the 1961 Experimental Edition. It has new norms and contains ten basic tests and two supplementary tests which are as follows.

Auditory reception. The child is required to give a yes or no answer to questions of increasing difficulty.

Visual reception. The child is shown a stimulus picture and asked to choose from four other pictures one conceptually similar.

Auditory vocal association. The child is asked to complete an analogy.

Visual Motor association. The child is asked to choose from four pictures, the one that 'goes with' the stimulus picture.

Verbal expression. The child is shown familiar objects and asked, 'Tell me about this'.

Manual expression. The child is shown common objects and asked, 'Show me what we do with this'.

Grammatical closure. The child is asked e.g. 'Here is a dog, there are two ——?'

Auditory closure. The child is asked to fill in the missing parts of a spoken word.

Sound blending. The child is asked to blend parts of a word spoken singly.

Visual closure. The child is required to identify a common object when only a part is visible.

Auditory sequential memory. The child is required to repeat a sequence of spoken digits.

Visual sequential memory. The child is required to reproduce from memory, a sequence of meaningless figures.

The results of this test are plotted on a graph to make a profile showing strengths and weaknesses. An account of remedial work based upon such profiles can be found in *The Diagnosis and Remediation of Psycholinguistic Abilities*, by S. A. Kirk, Institute for Research on Exceptional Children, University of Illinois.

Marianne Frostig Developmental Test of Visual Perception

3rd edition; 3 to 8 years; 1964; 30–35 minutes for individual test, 40 to 60 minutes for group; N.F.E.R. Test Agency.

This test is designed to measure certain kinds of visual perception in young children and to pinpoint the age at which they develop. There are five subtests: *eye-motor coordination* in which the child has to draw straight or curved lines between narrow limits; *figure-ground discrimination* which requires discrimination between intersecting shapes and finding hidden figure; *form constancy* requiring discrimination of squares and circles in different sizes and positions; *position in space*, in which the child has to differentiate between figures in an identical position and those in a rotated or reversed position;

spatial relations, in which the child has to copy patterns by joining dots.

It is useful as a screening test for young children who may need special training in visual perception, and it has been of benefit in the education of children with reading disabilities and brain injury.

Visual Motor Gestalt Test

4 to 11 years; 1946; untimed; L. Bender; N.F.E.R. Test Agency.

This test consists of nine cards each bearing a pattern which is to be copied by the child. The test provides a means of assessing the ability to reproduce the spatial relationships between intersecting wavy lines, oblique rows of dots, a contingent square and circle, etc. Norms are given for ages four to eleven. The test has been used to explore, among other disabilities, retardation, reading disabilities, brain-damage. See *Bender Gestalt Test for Young Children* by Koppitz for a scoring system.

The Harris Test of Lateral Dominance.

7 years to adult; 3rd edition; 1958; individual; A. J. Harris; N.F.E.R. Test Agency.

The test manual lists and describes the subtests entitled knowledge of left and right, hand preferences, simultaneous writing, handwriting, tapping, dealing cards, strength of grip, monocular tests, binocular tests, stereoscopic tests, foot dominance.

The apparatus required for the full test includes a telescope, kaleidoscope, rifle, playing cards, stereoscope, dynamometer, but useful information regarding a child's eyedness, footedness, handedness, can be gained by using the subtests that do not require expensive apparatus.

Two tables are provided giving age-trends in lateral dominance for children with reading disabilities and for an unselected group of children aged seven years and nine years. Separate norm-tables are provided for handwriting, tapping and dealing cards. All the data are based on American children and adults.

Lefthandedness

Suggestions for simple tests of lefthandedness and a discussion of its causes and treatment will be found in Burt's *The Backward Child* Chapter 10, and in *Lefthandedness* by Margaret Clark, U.L.P.

13

Tests of Number Readiness

Over fifty years ago Cyril Burt produced number tests for children below the educational age of five, but wrote of them: 'It proved impossible to base age-assignments solely upon the data obtained from normal children of four and five. Among children of such years, differences of teaching, in the schemes and methods in the infant department, . . . have a disproportionate influence and the results are equally capricious.'[1] Thus cautioned we may look at some examples from Burt's Oral Arithmetic Test.

Educational age of 4
How many fingers do I hold up? (showing two)
Count how many fingers there are now. (holding out our with each hand).
How many are 7 and 1 more?
If I gave you 3 sweets and you ate 2 how many would you have left?

Educational age of 5
What are twice two?
4 boys gave me a halfpenny each. How many pennies is that?
A boy caught 4 fish on Friday and 3 on Saturday. How many fish did he catch all together?

These questions are suggested as 'suitable for testing a sense of number'. They are not standardised upon the ages stated, but upon the replies of older dull children.

One would have expected that by now, over fifty years since Burt's early work, that Britain would possess properly standardised

[1] *Mental and Scholastic Tests*, p. 326.

tests of number readiness, but in fact very little progress has been made.

American number readiness tests

There are many group tests of number readiness which have been standardised on American kindergartern and first-grade children. Two of the most widely used are contained in the Metropolitan Readiness Tests and the Primary Mental Abilities Tests. The Metropolitan Number Readiness test consists of two subtests, numbers and copying. In the numbers subtest the child is shown rows of pictures or figures and is given instructions such as :'Put a mark on the bigger tree.' 'Cross out three horses.' In the copying sub-test the child is required to copy a variety of shapes, including a circle, triangle and diamond, and a number of capital letters and numbers.

The number-readiness test in the Primary Mental Abilities battery consists wholly of rows of pictures of familiar objects such as cakes, keys, soldiers, dolls, candles. The child's understanding of numbers and number vocabulary is tested by instructions such as:

Mark the two cakes that are closest together
Mark the largest doll and the smallest doll
Mark eleven keys
If I blow out six candles how many will still be lit?

British users of these tests should scrutinise them for Americanisms, (which in fact are very few) and note that the norms are based on the performance of American children.

In contrast to the number-readiness tests described above, which are chiefly concerned with number language, counting, and recognition of figures, a more recent trend has been to devise tests which assess fundamental concepts. These concepts are concerned with the child's ability to understand, e.g. that a given quantity of material does not change in amount even when it undergoes changes in shape (conservation); the relationships between the elements in a series (seriation); and that an object can belong at one and the same time to two different classes within a group (part- whole relationships).

116

Individual tests of number concepts

Experiments of this kind have led to a greater understanding of how a child's ideas about number relationships develop. Thanks largely to the work of Piaget and his many collaborators, teachers are becoming more concerned about a child's understanding of number relationships than about his ability to compute or remember tables. The most fruitful source of these experiments is the *Child's Conception of Number* by Jean Piaget, and in the following pages are a few suggestions culled from that book; these 'tests' are not standardised and yield no number age but they do throw light on the child's understanding of basic relationships concerning numbers.

Conservation

1. Put out two lines of sweets, saying 'one for you, one for me' and ensure that individual sweets are opposite those in the other row.

```
o   o   o   o   o   o   o   o   o   o
o   o   o   o   o   o   o   o   o   o
```

Now ask the child whether he has more, or you have more, or whether you both have the same number of sweets. If the child does not agree that you both have the same, reduce the numbers in each line until he does. Then close up one line of sweets and again ask the same question.

```
o    o    o    o    o    o    o    o    o    o
o o o o o o o o o o
```

Some children are deceived into thinking that because one row occupies a greater area than the other it contains more sweets. Such children are usually under six mentally. One may check a child's reaction by opening out the lower line and closing up the other line, then asking the question again. A child who is so deceived is not seeing the group as composed of several individual sweets but as an agglomeration; his judgement of content is based upon an overall impression rather than upon analysis of the parts.

The child may check the number of sweets in each line by

117

counting. Even with this evidence some children will still maintain that the amounts in the two lines are different. They see no contradiction. Later, perhaps at the mental age of about six-and-a-half to seven, the child may immediately reject the question as nonsensical. But what appears to him to be self-evident, that the number of items is not changed by their rearrangement, is a feat of understanding that his mind has achieved by working on experience during the previous few months.

The practical implication of this to the teacher is that a child cannot be expected to use symbols like six, eight, etc. sensibly if he feels that at any moment his six may become suddenly more or less, if he feels that numbers have no constancy, do not conserve their identity.

2. Another way of testing a child's ability to see a group as composed of separate units and at the same time as a global shape, is to present a simple shape made of counters and ask him to put down the same number of counters. Set out the counters on the shape of a ring or an L and say 'there are some counters for you. I want you to put down as many counters as I have put down'.

Models   Possible Copies

Children who have not reached the stage of analysing the group into its elements will copy the shape but ignore the exact number of counters.

3. It is only gradually that children learn to hold in their minds two qualities or aspects of a group at one and the same time. This is demonstrated by the now famous example of presenting the child with, say, twenty wooden beads, two of which are white, while the rest are brown, and the child is asked: 'Are there more brown beads than wooden beads?' At a certain stage of development the child cannot think of a bead as belonging to a wooden class and a brown class at the same time: either it belongs to the wooden class or to

the brown class. If he mentally separates the brown beads from the total group he must mentally remove the bead itself, woodenness and everything about it, and not simply the attributes of brownness.

4. Tell the child that he can have eight sweets for today, four for the morning session and four for the afternoon. Tomorrow he can have eight sweets but only one may be eaten in the morning and the others must be saved for the afternoon.

The sweets, or whatever represents them, may be set out in the following way.

	Morning	Afternoon
TODAY	o o	o o
	o o	o o
TOMORROW	o	o o o
		o o o o

The child is then asked whether he has more sweets to eat today than tomorrow, or whether he has more tomorrow, or whether he has the same number each day. At the lower level of ability the child's perception is dominated by the morning allotments or the afternoon allotments, so that he says either that today there will be more (because he is comparing four with one) or that tomorrow there will be more (because he is comparing seven with four). With experience the child becomes able to 'decentre' or shift his focus of perception freely from one part of the group to another, and to imagine the displaced three in their original position. The ability to imagine a displaced item or series of items back in the original position and to see the relationship between the two possible positions, is closely related to Piaget's notion of 'reversibility'.

5. Conservation of liquid and reversibility

Have two glass jars of the same shape and size containing lemonade, and adjust the contents until the child agrees that there is the same quantity in each. Call one yours and the other his. Pour the contents of his tall thin glass container and ask if he now has more, or if you have more, or if you both have the same. If the child thinks the respective amounts have now changed, questioning can reveal which dimension he is looking at, height or width, and which dimension he is ignoring. By pouring the contents of one jar into several smaller containers one may find that the child is influenced not only by height or width by also but the number of containers.

6. Dividing a group into halves

One of the insights a child gains when he masters the number-bonds that make ten is that one part of ten increases as its partner decreases, i.e. having said $8+2=10$ then the answer to $7+?=10$ must be 3 because having taken one from eight to make seven we must add one to two to compensate. Whether the child has this kind of insight can be demonstrated by the following test.

Put before the child two unequal groups of counters, say seven and eleven, and ask him to make the same number in each group by moving counters from one group to the other. Some children of infant age will begin transferring counters to the smaller group and be so oblivious of the effect on the other group as to reduce it to only one or two, then begin the process all over again in the reverse direction.

7. Ordination

It is sometimes assumed that because a child understands cardinal numbers he necessarily understands ordinal numbers: that a knowledge of six implies a knowledge of sixth. Children may well use the names third, fourth, etc. without really appreciating the meaning of these words. This understanding can be tested by making a staircase out of graded blocks, allowing a doll to 'climb' to, say, the fifth stair then asking the child how many single stairs like the first one (one unit), placed on top of each other, would reach as high as the stair the doll is on. A full understanding of the word 'fifth' should include an awareness that the fifth is the last of a group of five.

8. Seriation

The use of the staircase can also help to demonstrate a child's appreciation of the principle underlying a series. Having made a staircase from one to ten with graduated rods, remove two rods without the child seeing where they are taken from, say the fourth and the eighth, close up the remaining rods and ask the child to replace the two in their proper places. To do this the child must see that each stair is at once both smaller than one neighbour and larger than the other. Many infants can see only one relationship at a time.

None of the above tests need involve any writing or addition, subtraction, multiplication, division, yet they do test whether a child has grasped certain essential ideas about the relationships between numbers and about the nature of groups.

A selection of these simple tests could be given to infants on entry and at intervals thereafter to check progress.

14

Tests of Arithmetic and Mathematics

Tests of mechanical arithmetic

The Staffordshire Test of Computation

7 to 15 years; 1969 revision; untimed; M. E. Hebron; Harrap.

In this revision of the Staffordshire Arithmetic Test the money sums have been decimalised but metrication has not been adopted.

Nottingham Number Test

9.1 to 11.0 years; individual or group; 1973; W. E. C. Gillham and K. A. Hesse; U.L.P.

Designed for the level above that catered for by the same author's Leicester Number Test, it tests the basic number concepts and calculations, mainly series, place-value, and the four rules.

Leicester Number Test

7.1 to 9.0 years; 1973; untimed; W. E. C. Gillham and K. A. Hesse; U.L.P.

This is an extended and revised edition of the original test published in 1968, in that second-year junior norms have been added. It covers a range extending from the conservation of number and counting to fractions and simple computation.

Group Mathematics Test

6.6 to 12.11 years; 1970; two periods of 20 minutes; D. Young; U.L.P.

This is a test of mathematical understanding at a very simple level. It is suitable for children of a wide range of ability between 6.6 and 8.6 and for less able children up to the age of 12.11.

The test is on a sheet and has four subtests, two pictorial and orally administered, and two on mechanical addition and subtraction. The test was standardised in Yorkshire. There are two parallel forms.

Graded Arithmetic-Mathematics Test

7 to 21 years; 1963; timed 20 minutes; P. E. Vernon; U.L.P.

This test is unique in being constructed after the style of the Stanford-Binet Intelligence Scale, five scores being allotted to each year of age. Before giving the test, an estimate must be made of the child's ability, perhaps based on reading age or mental age, then the child is started at a little below this estimate. This would be used as an individual test since it would be difficult to administer it to a group whose members needed to start at varying levels. No conversion table is provided since the arithmetic-mathematics age is reckoned directly from the number of sums correct. Vernon suggests the use of Ballard's One Minute Arithmetic Tests to obtain a rough measure of arithmetic age among six- to seven-year-olds and quotes revised norms for the Ballard Tests.

This test is intended primarily for use in Educational and Child Guidance Clinics to be followed, in the event of serious backwardness, by diagnostic tests.

Mathematical Tests

Number Test D E

10½ to 12½ years; 1966; untimed, but approx. 50 minutes; group or individual; 50 items measuring an understanding of the four number processes. B. Barnard; Ginn for N.F.E.R.

This test marks a new departure in testing an understanding of arithmetical ideas. Two examples will suffice:

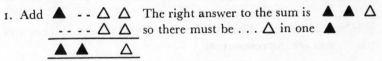

1. Add ▲ -- △ △   The right answer to the sum is ▲ ▲ △
      - - - - △ △   so there must be . . . △ in one ▲
      ▲ ▲   △

2. Three white circles equal one black circle   ○ ○ ○ = ●
   Three black circles equal one white square   ● ● ● = □
   How many times greater is □ than ○ ?

The test measures an understanding of number processes rather than an ability to compute, and is offered as suitable for sorting out arithmetic groups in the first year of the secondary school.

Mathematics Attainment Test C1

9.3 to 10.8 years; 1966; untimed but approx. 50 minutes; Ginn for N.F.E.R.

This test was constructed by a group of Surrey primary school teachers and was designed to measure understanding of mathematics rather than computational skill. The fifty items include problems on graphs, deciding which process to use, fractions, factors, time and area.

Mathematics Attainment Test C3

9.3 to 10.8 years; 1966; untimed, but approx. 50 minutes; Ginn for N.F.E.R.

This was constructed by a group of Middlesex teachers and tests understanding rather than computational skill. The fifty items include problems on fractions, graphs, place value, series, estimates.

Mathematics Attainment Test B (Oral)

8.6 to 9.8 years; 1965; untimed but approx. 45 minutes; Ginn for N.F.E.R.

This was constructed by a group of Worcestershire teachers to test the mathematical experience and understanding of second-year juniors. The group also carried out an enquiry to see whether administering the test orally produced different results from those obtained when the test was given non-orally. Using two groups matched for reading ability and age, one group doing the oral version and the other group doing the non-oral, it was found that both poor readers and good readers showed a significant increase in score.

The forty-two items include questions on estimates, fractions, graphs, volume, area. Since the test is orally administered it requires particular care in presentation.

Mathematics Attainment Test A (Oral)

7 to 8.6 years; 1970; untimed but takes about 45 minutes; Ginn for N.F.E.R.

The items are all in the form of problems to be dictated, illustrated by well spaced drawings. The knowledge tested includes arithmetic vocabulary, four rules, inserting the missing sign, number bonds.

Mathematics Test D E 1

10 to 12 years; 1967; untimed but about 50 minutes; Ginn for N.F.E.R.

This is a 45 item test that has been modified since its original standardisation to meet the demands of decimalisation and metrication.

Mathematics Test D E 2

10 to 11.11 years; 1969; untimed but about 50 minutes; Ginn for N.F.E.R.

This is a 46 item test testing the understanding of mathematical concepts, fully recognising the introduction of decimalisation and metrication.

Basic Mathematics Tests A and B

7.0 to 8.0 years (A) and 8.0 to 9.0 years (B); 1973; 1 hour; Ginn for N.F.E.R.

Both these tests cover a range of mathematical skills provided by 40 items that yield valuable diagnostic information.

Basic Mathematics Test C

10 to 12.6 years; 1969; untimed but about 50 minutes; Ginn for N.F.E.R.

Questions include items on area graphs, symmetry, sets, decimals and fractions.

Basic Mathematics Test D E

10 to 12.6 years; untimed but about 50 minutes; Ginn for N.F.E.R.

This test contains 55 items on symmetry, tabulation, fractions, algebra, spatial ability, graphs, etc.

Basic Mathematics Test F G

12.6 to 14.6 years; 1969; untimed but about 50 minutes; Ginn for N.F.E.R.

This test is designed to assess a wide range of mathematical concepts.

Decimal Currency Test

This is intended to test the ability to understand decimal currency and is for children of any age. No norms have been made since it will obviously be of transient value. It requires a reading-age of about nine and takes about an hour.

Diagnostic tests of arithmetic

Schonell Diagnostic Arithmetic Tests

7 to 15 years; Test 1936, Manual 1957; 12 subtests timed or untimed; F. J. Schonell; Oliver and Boyd.

Tests 1 to 5 include all the basic number combinations in the four basic processes. Tests 6 to 11 give all the steps, in order of difficulty in addition, subtraction, multiplication, short and long division. Test 12 consists of forty items of graded mental arithmetic in problem form involving the four rules, money, weight and length and was written long before decimalisation was introduced. For purely diagnostic purposes the tests are given in unlimited time, but norms are given for timed testing should these be required.

Diagnostic Tests in Vulgar Fractions, Decimal Fractions and Percentages

11 to 14 years; 1956; timed or untimed; 25 minutes for each of three tests; F. J. Schonell, J. Richardson, K. P. O'Connor; Oliver and Boyd.

The test on vulgar fractions has separate sections on each of the four rules; the test on decimal fractions has separate sections on changing vulgar fractions to decimal fractions, changing decimal fractions to vulgar fractions, arranging decimals in order of magnitude, and a section on the four rules. The test on percentages has sections on changing decimal and vulgar fractions to percentages, changing percentages to vulgar and decimal fractions, finding percentages of numbers and quantities, expressing one number or quantity as a percentage of another, and finding the full value of numbers and quantities when a percentage is given.

One of the most valuable parts of the handbook is an analysis of the errors made by children in these particular processes.

Primary Mathematics Diagnostic Tests

10+ years; 1966; untimed; J. S. Flavell and R. B. Wakelam; Methuen.

This consists of two sheets, Test 1 and Test 2. Test 1, headed Notation, deals with principles underlying notations, e.g. what is 2 worth in the numbers 702, 1234, 6025? Test 2 is headed Translation, and requires the pupil to translate verbal problems into mathematical language. The tests discover weaknesses in pupils' understanding of mathematical language.

Class analysis charts

Any arithmetic test that contains a fair number of well-graded items can be used diagnostically if the results are entered on a class-analysis sheet such as the one on p. 128.

A chart of this kind will enable the teacher to organise remedial groups quickly, and if such a chart is compiled at suitable intervals then progress can be instantly seen both for individuals and the class as a whole.

CLASS ANALYSIS CHART

Type of process

Child	u+u no c.f.	u+u c.f.	u+t.u. no c.f.	t.u.+t.u. c.f.	t.u.−t.u. no c.f.	t.u.−t.u. c.f.
J.F.	√	√	√	√	√	×
R.H.	×	×	×	×	×	×
E.U.	√	×	√	×	√	×
S.G.	√	√	√	√	√	v
D.G.	√	√	√	√	√	√
R.X.	√	√	√	×	√	×
E.Y.	√	√	√	√	√	×
G.T.	√	√	√	√	√	√
A.C.	√	×	√	×	√	×
T.S.	√	√	√	√	√	×
Totals	1	3	1	4	1	7

It can be seen that seven children need help with sums subtracting tens and units from tens and units where there is a carrying figure, four need help in adding tens and units to tens and units when there is a carrying figure, etc., etc.

15

Tests of English

The N.F.E R. English Progress Tests were designed to provide a continuous assessment of English skill from seven to fourteen years. Unlike many of the tests of reading and number, none of these is timed.

English Progress Test A
8 to 9.0 years; 1952; a average time 40 minutes; 4 sections each of 10 items concerned with common combinations of words, class names, understanding of a short story, and written answers to everyday questions; A. F. Watts; Ginn for N.F.E.R.

English Progress Test B
9.0 to 10.2 years; 1952; average time 40 minutes; 50 items including reading comprehension, written expression, punctuation, spelling, grammatical usage; M. A. Brimer; Ginn for N.F.E.R.

English Progress Test C
10 to 11.0 years; 1952; average time 45 to 50·minutes; 50 items on vocabulary, tense sequence, reading for meaning, completing statements, re-expression of simple sentences; A. F. Watts; Ginn for N.F.E.R.

English Progress Test D
11 to 12 years; 1955; average time 40 to 45 minutes; 60 items covering vocabulary, comprehension, expression, grammatical usage, punctuation, spelling; M. A. Brimer; Ginn for N.F.E.R.

English Progress Test E

12 to 13 years; 1955; average time 40 to 45 minutes, similar to Test D; M. A. Brimer; Ginn for N.F.E.R.

English Progress Test F

13 to 14 years; 1953; average time 45 minutes; 85 items covering sentence completion, finding the middle term, and vocabulary; Ginn for N.F.E.R.

English Test F G

12 to 13.11 years; 1952; 1 hour; 120 items on vocabulary selection and invention, reported speech, grammatical usage, knowledge of idiom, sentence joining, punctuation, comprehension, poetry completion, spelling, dictionary usage; G. A. V. Morgan; Ginn for N.F.E.R.

Designed to cover the common content of English teaching in the secondary modern school.

The series of English tests A2 to F2 and G, has been constructed to reflect modern English teaching. The emphasis is on encouraging a free response rather than on requiring an answer to a multiple choice question.

English Progress A2

7.3 to 8.11 years; 1965; untimed but approximately 50 minutes; items on rhymes, plurals, spelling, vocabulary, processes, tenses, comprehension; B. Barnard; Ginn for N.F.E.R.

English Progress B2

$8\frac{1}{2}$ to 10 years; 1960; untimed but approximately 40 minutes; 45 items on rhyming, opposites, plurals, past tense, comprehension, punctuation, sentence completion; Ginn for N.F.E.R.

English Progress Test B3

8 to 9.6 years; untimed but about 45 minutes; Ginn for N.F.E.R.

This 40-item test includes items on classification of words, synonyms, comprehension, and is a multiple-choice test.

English Progress C2

$9\frac{1}{2}$ to 11 years; 1960; untimed; approximately 40 minutes. 54 items

on comprehension, synonyms, punctuation, spelling, elaborating
sentences, past and present tense, sentence completion, paragraph
titles; V. Land; Ginn for N.F.E.R.

English Progress D2

10½ to 12 years; 1964; untimed, approximately 45 minutes; 75 items
on converting verbs to nouns, sentence sequence, comprehension,
words for phrases, sentence completion, personal pronouns, spelling,
conjunctions, punctuation, sentence construction; J. Henchman;
Ginn for N.F.E.R.

English Progress Test B

9 to 10.6 years; untimed, about 40 minutes; Ginn for N.F.E.R.
   The test includes items on punctuation, spelling, comprehension,
and grammatical usage.

English Progress Test D3

10 to 11.6 years; untimed, about 45 minutes; Ginn for N.F.E.R.
   A 50 item test of the ability to use words that are contextually
correct and to understand the meaning of both prose and poetry.

English Progress E2

11 to 13 years; 1962; untimed, approximately 45 minutes; 70 items
on personal pronouns, sentence completion, words for phrases,
apostrophes, comprehension, proverbs, verb forms, sentence
arrangement, punctuation; S. W. Unwin; Ginn for N.F.E.R.

English Progress F2

12 to 13½ years; 1963; untimed, approximately 45 minutes; 60 items
on comprehension, spelling, sentence completion, punctuation,
writing a paragraph, sentence sequence, gender, abstract nouns;
J. Henchman and E. Hendry; Ginn for N.F.E.R.

English Progress Test F3

12 to 13.6 years; untimed, about 45 minutes; Ginn for N.F.E.R.
   The content is similar to that of English Progress Test D3.
Provisionally standardised in 1969.

English Progress Test G

13½ to 15 years; 1962; untimed, approximately 40 minutes. 60 items on plurals, prepositions, comprehension, direct and indirect speech, rearranging sentences, words for phrases, sentence completion, converting verbs to nouns and nouns to verbs, spelling and punctuation; S. M. Unwin; Ginn for N.F.E.R.

Cotswold Junior Ability Tests, English, Series A to F

9 to 10½ years; 1950 to 1961; 6 timed subtests totalling 35 minutes; each test contains items on reading comprehension, word usage, composition, spelling, sentence structure, and a practice page; group or individual; A and B are for 9-year-olds, C and D for 8½- to 9½-year-olds, and E and F for 9½- to 10½-year-olds; no information on reliability or validity; C. M. Fleming; Gibson.

Cotswold Measurement of Ability, English, Series 1 to 12

10 to 13 years; 1950–1964; each test contains timed subtests totalling 35 to 40 minutes; group or individual; similar in content to the Junior Ability Tests but at a higher level; C. M. Fleming; Gibson.

Clerical Test F G

12.0 to 13.11 years; 1 hour; group or individual; Ginn for N.F.E.R.

This is designed to discover those children who have potential ability for clerical courses and contains subtests on indexing, checking, decoding, classification, message decoding.

Spelling Tests

Kelvin Measurement of Spelling Ability

7½ to 12½ years; group or individual; 133; untimed; C. M. Fleming; Gibson.

This consists of sixty sentences each with a word missing. As a sentence is dictated the child reads it and then writes in the missing word. Spelling ages, standardised scores and percentiles are given.

Grade Word Spelling Test

5 to 12.3 years; 1958; untimed; group or individual; Daniels and Diack; Chatto and Windus.

This consists of four sets of ten words each set being of a particular kind of construction. The child writes each word as it is dictated. Spelling ages are given, but there is no evidence of validity or reliability. The test is contained in *Standard Reading Tests*.

Graded Word Spelling Test A and B

5 to 15 years; 1945; untimed; group or individual; F. Schonell; Oliver and Boyd.

This consists of a hundred words dictated by the teacher, and to be written by the child, each set of ten words representing one year of spelling age. The two tests are of comparable difficulty. No evidence of reliability or validity is given.

16

Test Batteries

When a child has been tested on several standardised tests, e.g. reading, spelling, general ability, and differences are found between his various scores, it is often quite wrongly assumed that these differences reflect real differences in his abilities. It is not uncommon to find a child's profile being plotted from results on Schonell's Spelling Test, the Stanford Binet Intelligence Scale, the Burt Reading Test, and the Staffordshire Arithmetic Test, without an awareness that the child is being compared, (*a*) with a small number of English children of the 1940's for spelling, (*b*) a large number of American children of the 1950's for intelligence, (*c*) a sample of Glasgow children of the 1930's for reading, and a thousand Staffordshire children of the 1950's for arithmetic. Scores derived from such a motley collection of tests are clearly not strictly comparable.

A child's various abilities can be validly compared with each other only if the tests used have all been standardised on the same population at roughly the same time, and on children whose learning opportunities have been similar to those of the child being tested. Many local education authorities commission such test-batteries for their own use but teachers rarely use test-batteries for their own children. The following are available to any school.

France Wiseman Educational Guidance Programme

7.6 to 11.1 years; 1964; group, except for reading-test; untimed; N. France and S. Wiseman; Collins.

The stated intention of this programme is to provide a cumulative description of the whole child, enabling the teacher to see where remedial training is required, or where the teacher is paying too much attention to a particular subject. There are three booklets: 1A for ages 7.6 to 9.1 years; 2A for ages 9.2 to 10.1 years; and 3A for ages 10.2 to 11.1 years. Each contains subtests on comprehension, vocabulary, verbal reasoning, puzzles, addition-subtraction, multiplication-division, spelling, reading, as well as devices for sampling the child's likes and dislikes and gaining information about his family.

Each subtest is separately scorable in terms of standard scores, and the handbook gives typical profiles with comments on the possible causes and recommended treatment. The whole programme was standardised in November 1964 in Warwickshire and Solihull.

Bristol Achievement Tests

8 to 13.11 years; 1968; group; three junior tests 50 minutes; two senior tests 55 minutes; two parallel forms; A. Brimer; Nelson.

This battery is claimed by the authors to measure achievement in English, Maths and Study Skills, whatever the form of teaching or content of syllabus a school may use. Separate tests on each topic for each year are provided as follows: Level 1, 2nd year junior, age 8 to 9.11 years; Level 2, 3rd year junior, age 9 to 10.11 years; Level 3, 4th year junior, age 10 to 11.11 years; Level 4, 1st year secondary, age 11 to 12.11 years; Level 5, 2nd year secondary, age 12 to 13.11 years.

The overlapping of age groups between one level and another is deliberate to allow for length of schooling: thus although a 10 year-old would be in both the 2nd and 3rd year age groups the choice of giving either Level 3 or Level 4 tests would depend upon the class he was in, i.e. his length of schooling.

Each subject has five parts, separately assessable. The English test is divided into word-meaning, paragraph meaning, sentence organisation, organisation of ideas, spelling and punctuation; Maths into number, reasoning, space, measurement, arithmetic laws and processes; Study Skills into properties, structures, processes, explanations, interpretations.

The tests were all standardised within the same four weeks thus making possible a valid comparison between the child's performance on the various topics. The fact that the tests measure the same function at each level enables a longitudinal record of the child's progress to be made.

The administrative manual advises on how to record score-profiles which include the plotting of standard errors for each score, a very valuable corrective to those who think five or six points between standard scores reflects a real difference in ability.

17

Tests of Social Adaptation, Aptitude, Interest and Personality

Vineland Social Maturity Scale
0 to 25 years; 1947; individual; untimed; E. A. Doll; N.F.E.R. Test Agency.

The scale consists of 117 brief statements describing social skills and behaviour, and arranged to represent increasing levels of social maturity. The aspects of social maturity covered are: self-help, locomotion, occupation, self-direction, socialisation and communication. The scale is claimed to be useful as a statement of normal development, as a tool for measuring social retardation, and for measuring the effects of a course of treatment. Doll stresses that the tester should devote 'at least as much care to mastering the technique as that required for administering the Binet scale'. The norms are American.

The Manchester Scales of Social Adaptation
6 to 15 years; 1966; individual; E. A. Lunzer; N.F.E.R. Test Agency, Level P.

This test has been developed from the Vineland Social Maturity Scale to provide a measure suitable for English children. There are two sections, social perspective and self-direction, described by Lunzer as 'know that' and 'know how' respectively. The first section is concerned with general matters (e.g. name and address, birthday), sport, current affairs, aesthetic topics, scientific topics; the second section is concerned with play, freedom of movement, self-help, handling money, and responsibility in the home. The scales were standardised on children in the Manchester and Cheshire area and are regarded by the author as provisional, to be revised and extended in due course. Raw scores are convertible to percentile scores for each year of age.

Bristol Social Adjustment Guides

5 to 16 years; 1971; untimed; individual; D. H. Stott and N. C. Marston; U.L.P.

The purpose of these Guides is to detect and diagnose maladjustment, unsettledness or other emotional handicap. There are three Guides entitled respectively, *The Child in School, The Child in Residential Care* and *The Child in the Family*. References here are confined to the *Child in School Guide* since that is the one most commonly used and the general procedure for each of the forms is very much the same. Each Guide consists of a number of statements about a child's behaviour in a variety of situations and the statements are grouped under headings such as 'Interaction with Teacher', 'School Work', 'Games and Play', 'Personal Ways'.

The person completing the Guide underlines for each situation the statement that best describes the child's behaviour. For example, under the section 'Interaction with Teacher' the statements concerned with 'greeting teacher' are: waits to be noticed / hails teacher loudly / greets normally / can be surly / never thinks of greeting / is too unaware of people to greet / nothing noticeable.

When the underlining is completed a transparent template marked only with items that indicate some kinds of emotional disturbance, is then placed over each page of the Guide. Those underlined items that coincide with the template items are then recorded on a Diagnostic Form which is arranged in such a way as to reveal clearly the extent and the nature of the child's disturbance.

It is not suggested that the Guide should be completed for all children. Stott recommends, however, that a teacher might answer six 'Adjustment Pointers' for each child in the class and that this quick survey would show which children deserved an analysis by the use of one of the Guides. The 'Adjustment Pointers' are six questions that require a mere 'yes' or 'no' answer.

Use of the Guides is explained in Stott's *The Social Adjustment of Children*, 4th edition 1971 (U.L.P.), and accounts of their application to actual cases are given in his *Unsettled Children and Their Families* (U.L.P.).

Delinquency Prediction Instrument
1961; untimed; individual; D. H. Stott; U.L.P.

In a survey of all the boys placed on probation in Glasgow for the first time during 1957, Dr Stott assessed the extent of their behaviour-disturbance by means of the Bristol Social Adjustment Guides. He found that in comparison with a control group of non-delinquent boys of the same age and attending the same school they contained a high proportion of maladjusted and unsettled boys.

The behaviour patterns of these boys, as shown on the Guides, showed that fifty-four items occurred at least four times as often among the delinquents as among the non-delinquents. These fifty-four items form the basis of the Delinquency Prediction Instrument. To use the Instrument the Guide is filled in in the usual way, the items transferred to the Diagnostic Form, then the Delinquency Prediction Key, which is a transparent form on which are printed the fifty-four items, is placed on top of the Diagnostic Form and lined up so that it can be seen which underlined items coincide with the 'delinquency' items. The number and nature of the delinquency items underlined gives a measure of proneness to delinquency.

Progress Assessment Charts
Birth to adult; Forms 1 and 2, 1965, Primary Form, 1966; Form 1A, 1973; individual; H. Gunzburg; N.A.M.H.

These charts are intended for use with subnormal children and adults in training centres. The Primary Form is intended for use with babies, mentally handicapped children and severely mentally handicapped adults. Form 1 is intended for use with those having I.Q.s below 55; Form 2 applies primarily to young people within the range 55 to 80+ I.Q. Form 1A was devised to fill the gaps found to exist between levels 1 and 2.

The charts are designed to give a visual check of progress in the four main areas of development: self-help, communication, occupation, socialisation. After checking on the printed list of skills (e.g. assists in getting dressed, matches colours, asks to go to toilet) the results are transferred to a circular chart divided into quarters, each quarter representing one of the four main areas of development noted above. Each skill is represented by a space in the appropriate quarter, and when these spaces are shaded in for a particular person an immediate picture of that person's relative development is seen.

Sociometric testing

Sociometric testing takes a variety of forms, and may be used for many different purposes. Basically, the intention is to discover interrelationships between the members of a class and this is done by asking the pupils with whom they would like to be in certain situations. Knowing the social groupings in a class can help a teacher to use the natural leaders, to help the child who has no friends, to organise cooperative work-groups, and improve the social climate of the class.

While day-to-day observation by the teacher may reveal who are the inseparable friends, who is isolated, etc., a great deal more can be learned by the use of sociometric techniques. The following describes a very simple method used in an actual enquiry.

The children were asked to answer the following questions:

1. If you were moving to another class which three children would you choose to go with you? 1.   2.   3.
2. If you were having a special drama lesson which three people would you like to work with you? 1.   2.   3.
3. If you were going on a picnic which three children would you like to come with you? 1.   2.   3.
4. If you were going to a sports meeting which three children would you like to be with you? 1.   2.   3.

When the answers were collected they were then plotted on a chart to show the general pattern of choices. To show every choice in the form of a line from chooser to chosen would produce a bewildering maze. In the figure below only the strong choices are shown, i.e. where a child has chosen the same classmate for the four occasions. The girls have been put to one side and the boys on the other to bring out any cross-sex choices; obviously the chart could be divided according to, say, religion, colour, place of residence, to show relationships between these factors and friendships. The figures indicate the number of choices received.

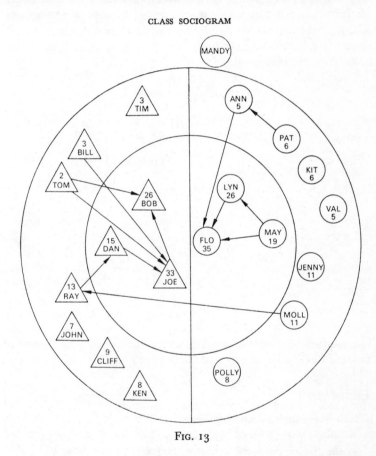

CLASS SOCIOGRAM

FIG. 13

It can be seen at a glance that the favourites are Joe and Flo, that Mandy and Tom will need help to gain acceptance by the rest of the class, and that there is only one 'strong' cross-sex choice.

It has to be remembered that these choices may not represent the actual friendships; some will, but others, e.g. Tom's choice of Joe, probably indicates only a wish for friendship. Neither is this situation to be assumed to be anything but temporary, especially as the pupils are young.

The detailed relationships between an individual child and her or his friends can be brought out by the use of personal sociograms. Kit, e.g. who has no strong choices on the class sociogram, nevertheless has friends among both boys and girls and three of her friendships are reciprocal.

PERSONAL SOCIOGRAM

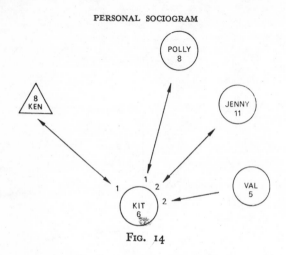

Fig. 14

The simplest of introductions to sociometric testing is *Sociometric Testing* bt M. L. Northway and L. Weld (O.U.P.).

Aptitude tests

D.T.B. Mechanical Ability Test
11 to adult; 1955; timed 15 minutes; individual or group; J. R. Morrisby, 6 Ben Austins, Rebourn, Herts.

The test consists of a number of drawings featuring, e.g. interlocking cog-wheels, see-saws, pulleys, about which the child has to make inferences using certain mechanical principles. The problems have been chosen to test 'natural mechanical aptitude' rather than learned principles of mechanics. General norms are given as well as norms for grammar schools and university students.

A.C.E.R. Mechanical Reasoning Test

13 to adult; 1951–54; 20 minutes; group or individual; N.F.E.R. Test Agency.

The test booklet contains twenty-four illustrated mechanical problems involving levers, pivots, pulleys, cams, etc., the correct answers to which have to be selected from four alternatives. The norms are Australian.

Prognostic Test of Mechanical Abilities

This test is useful for selecting students for trade-training, and contains subtests on arithmetic, reading drawings, identifying tools, spatial relationships, and checking measurements. Wrightsone and O'Toole; N.F.E.R. Test Agency.

Spatial Test 3

10 to 11.3 years; 1958; 30 minutes; Macfarlane Smith and J. S. Lawes; Ginn for N.F.E.R.

This is intended to help in the selection of students taking courses where an aptitude for visualising and manipulating shapes or patterns is important. Despite the age stated above, it has been found useful in colleges of further education. This test can only be ordered through Chief Education Officers.

Wing standardised tests of musical intelligence

8 to adult; 1939–58; individual or group; 50 to 60 minutes; H. D. Wing; N.F.E.R. Test Agency.

The test is on recording-tape and consists of standardised are tests including analysis of chords, pitch discrimination, memory for pitch, appreciation of harmony, intensity, rhythm and phrasing. The music is played on a piano. Results are given as gradings according to age, and may be useful in selecting pupils for school orchestras or for acceptance on a course of instruction in music.

Diagnostic Tests of Achievement in Music

9 to adult; 1950; 60 minutes; group or individual; M. L. Kotick and T. L. Torgenson. N.F.E.R. Test Agency.

This American test is in the form of a test booklet and is designed to test the extent of mastery of theory and skills which are involved in reading music and necessary for a musical education. There are ten parts to the test, i.e. diatonic syllable names; chromatic syllable names; number names; time signatures; major and minor keys; note and rest values; letter names; signs and symbols; key names; song recognition. There are two equivalent forms of the test.

Seashore Measures of Musical Talents
13 to adult; 1939; 1 hour; individual or group; C. E. Seashore; N.F.E.R. Test Agency.

These tests are on records and measure pitch, loudness, time, timbre, rhythm and tonal memory. The norms are American.

Measure of Musical Ability
7 to adult; 1966; 20 minutes; group or individual; A. Bentley; Harrap.

Shorter and simpler than the music tests noted above, this is produced on a 10″ long-playing record and consists of four sub-tests, pitch discrimination, tonal memory, chord analysis, and rhythm memory. The norms are British. A full account of its construction is in *Musical Ability in Children and its Measurement* by A. Bentley (Harrap).

Tests for Colour Blindness
5 to adult; 1964; individual; S. Ishihara; H. K. Lewis.

This consists of thirty-eight plates each showing a circular mosaic of colour in which is outlined a numeral or line in a particular colour or combination of colours. Weaknesses in colour discrimination are revealed by an inability to distinguish the numerals or lines. The particular plate that is misread provides a guide to the specific kind of colour-vision weakness. In large surveys only six of the plates need to be used, but failure on any of these warrants a testing on the full series.

Farnsworth Dichotomous Test of Colour Blindness
This test is designed to discriminate between those who are functionally colour blind and those who have moderately defective

colour-vision. It consists of a rack of fifteen colour caps which have to be arranged in order. Administration and scoring takes under 5 minutes. D. Farnsworth; N.F.E.R. Test Agency.

Devon Interest Test

11 to 13 years; 1955; group or individual; untimed; S. Wiseman and J. F. Fitzpatrick; Oliver and Boyd.

This consists of two questionnaires, one for boys and one for girls, designed to discover whether a child has an academic or a practical bias. The child is asked to state his or her preferences for certain occupations. The statements are in groups and each group contains six items composed of two practical, two academic, one social and one distractor. A typical group of items for girls is: doing embroidery, having no mistakes in written work, looking after pets, planning meals, finding new words in a dictionary, not letting the gang down.

The test has been found useful in helping towards the selection of pupils for grammar and technical education. The manual describes how the test was evolved and gives a frank account of its limitations.

Cotswold Personality Assessment, P.A.1

11 to 16 years; 1960; untimed, approximately 40 minutes; group or individual; C. M. Fleming; Gibson.

This test attempts to assess personal characteristics as revealed through interests and values. The child is asked to show, by giving marks from 0 to 4, the degree of his agreement with statements such as: 'I enjoy getting my hands dirty'. 'I am never happy when alone'. 'I am no use in school', 'I wish for a chance to do research'. The items are under sections headed: knowing your own mind, talking about wishes, judging other people, choosing work, spending money, using one's hands, being with other people, talking about school, keeping a record.

Total scores show the child's relative preference for people, things, ideas.

Schedule D, for Recording Interest of Backward Pupils

1948; F. J. Schonell; Oliver and Boyd.

In his suggestions for teaching backward children, Schonell included a list of questions designed to discover the child's interests, the purpose being to give evidence of the child's character and give a useful indication of the kind of remedial material that might be effective. Schedule D is simply a list of eighteen questions concerning the child's favourite lessons, hobbies, games, ambitions, etc., and will be found on page 115 in *Backwardness in the Basic Subjects* (Oliver and Boyd).

Rothwell-Miller Interest Blank
N.F.E.R. Test Agency [Level P]

This has been developed to assess the vocational interests of school leavers and adults. The test material consists of a sheet on which are grouped nine lists of occupations. The subject is asked to state his order of preference in each list. There are separate sheets for males and females. The manual is extremely detailed in its descriptions of the application of the Blank to a variety of subjects.

A.P.U. Occupational Interests Guide
1970; S. J. Closs; U.L.P.

The purpose of this is similar to that of the Rothwell-Miller Blank. Its format is also similar in that there is a sheet to be completed; one for males and a different one for females. In the A.P.U. Guide, however, the subject is presented with 112 pairs of statements and asked to indicate which one in each pair he or she would prefer. E.g. (*a*) Solve algebra problems; (*b*) Make dressing gowns.

There is a stencil for marking responses. The manual can be issued only to approved users.

Junior Eysenck Personality Inventory
7 to 16 years; 1965; untimed; S. B. G. Eysenck; U.L.P.

The inventory, consisting of sixty questions requiring 'yes' or 'no' answers, measures two traits, i.e. extraversion-introversion and stability-instability. Marking is facilitated by a stencil. The Inventory was standardised on London and Rotherham children. This is a restricted test.

The New Junior Maudsley Inventory

9+ years; 1966; untimed; W. D. Furneaux and H. B. Gibson; U.L.P.

The purpose of this inventory is the same as that of the Junior Eysenck Personality Inventory; namely to measure the two factors of extraversion—introversion and neuroticism-stability. It consists of 64 statements to which the child is invited to say whether he agrees or disagrees. A lie scale is incorporated. Restricted test.

High School Personality Questionnaire (H.S.P.Q.)

11 to 18 years; 2nd edition 1963; untimed but about 50 minutes; parallel forms A and B; group; R. B. Cattell; N.F.E.R. Test Agency; Level Q.

The H.S.P.Q. consists of a booklet of 142 questions to which the subject is invited to answer 'yes', 'no', or 'perhaps'. It is intended to measure fourteen distinct dimensions of personality and thus provide information on which to base predictions regarding vocational fitness, delinquency, leadership, etc. A profile is obtained showing the subject's placing on factors such as reserved-warmhearted; dull-bright, obedient-assertive, relaxed-tense.

Children's Personality Questionnaire (C.P.Q.)

8 to 12 years; 1963; parallel forms A and B; group; R. B. Cattell; N.F.E.R Test Agency; Level Q.

Each of the two forms is divided into two parts, each part requiring about 30-40 minutes to administer. The test measures the same fourteen factors as does the H.S.P.Q.

Early School Personality Questionnaire (E.S.P.Q.)

6 to 8 years; 1966; group; 2 parts, each 30–50 minutes; R. B. Cattell; N.F.E.R. Test Agency; Level Q.

This is an extension downwards of the C.P.Q. but with the important difference that the questions are read aloud to the class and the child marks his response on a sheet where the items are identified by pictures of coloured objects. The E S.P.Q. yields scores on thirteen dimensions of personality.

147

Sixteen Personality Factor Questionnaire (16 P.F.)

This American questionnaire which yields profiles based on the measurement of sixteen personality factors has now been standardised on British subjects, and the 1969 Supplement of Norms gives information on personality differences between British and American populations. This is a restricted test, available from the N.F.E.R. Test Agency.

Appendix 1

Tips for testers

Preliminary

1. Before deciding to use a test, be sure you know why you want to use it. What use will you make of the results?

2. Try the test yourself to be sure you know how to give it.

3. Choose the date and time of testing, ensuring that the session will not be interrupted by routine school events.

4. Obtain two or three more than you need of test copies and be sure you have a stop-watch and marking stencils if these are required.

5. Enlist and advise a colleague to assist with supervision.

On the day of testing

1. Put up warning sign: 'Do not disturb!'

2. Ensure assisting colleague is available and informed.

3. Ensure placing of seats prohibits copying.

4. Have a reserve of pencils.

5. Be sure you have allowed time for practice items and/or instructions as well as the working-time of the test.

6. Admit pupils at least five minutes before you are due to start.

7. Without encouraging a mass exodus allow pupils to go to lavatory.

8. Keep strictly to the test-instructions.

9. If some pupils are likely to finish early, announce before the test what you want them to do on finishing.

10. Before releasing pupils, ensure that every test-sheet has the pupils' name and personal details filled in.

Appendix 2

Many teachers who are too busy to consider the more complicated aspects of statistics find that simple correlation is both useful and easy to work out. Changes in pupils' scores on the same test on successive occasions are more vividly summed up by a correlation figure than by an inspection of actual scores or of rank orders. Finding the correlation between two sets of scores, say between the Deeside Picture Test and reading ability, or between a test of mathematics and one of music, leads to a sharper appreciation of the nature of each test and how far they may be testing the same thing.

The two types of correlation worked out below are rank correlation and product-moment correlation. Rank correlation is the simpler to calculate. The two sets of scores are arranged in rank order, each pupil's rankings in the two tests are compared in a systematic way, and an estimate of the general change in rank order is arrived at.

Product-moment correlation is used for more exact work and gives a more precise result. Most of the correlations quoted in test manuals are of the product-moment type. Instead of rankings, account is taken of the actual scores and of the scatter about the mean.

The value of knowing how to work out an average or a standard deviation becomes obvious when there is a need to compare a child's scores made on different tests. If Mr Smith has set one test and Mr Jones another, with little discussion as to the range of the scores and difficulty of the items, it would be imperative to find the standard deviation of each set of scores before individual pupils' scores on the two tests could be sensibly compared.

Rank correlation

To find the rank correlation between two sets of scores made by 10 pupils.

1. Opposite each pupil's name write his two scores as their rank order, i.e. 1st or 2nd or 3rd etc.

	PUPILS										
	A	B	C	D	E	F	G	H	I	J	
Test 1	8	3	9	2	7	10	4	6	1	5	} Ranking
Test 2	9	5	10	1	8	7	3	4	2	6	

2. Write the difference between each pupil's rankings on Test 1 and Test 2.

A	B	C	D	E	F	G	H	I	J
1	2	1	1	1	3	1	2	1	1

3. Square each difference and add

$$1+4+1+1+1+9+1+4+1+1=24$$

4. Apply the formula:

$$1 - \frac{6 \times \text{sum of the squared differences}}{\text{Number of items (No. of items}^2-1)}$$

$$1 - \frac{6 \times 24}{10\,(10^2-1)} = 1 - \frac{144}{990} = \cdot 85$$

The correlation between the two sets of scores is ·85 and is therefore reasonably high.

Rank correlation formula is usually given as $\quad 1 - \dfrac{6\,\Sigma\,d^2}{N\,(N^2-1)}$

Product moment correlation

1. Write the two sets of raw scores as in the 2nd and 3rd columns below putting the average for each set at the bottom.

2. In the fourth column write the differences between each of the scores in column X and the average for that column: thus 1 minus 7 is —6, and 3 minus 7 is —4, etc.

3. In the fifth column write the differences between each of the scores in the Y column and the average for that column: thus 1 minus 5 is —4, and 2 minus 5 is —3, etc.

4. In the column headed x^2 write the squares of each of the items in column x; in the column headed y^2 write the squares of each item in the y column.

5. In the column headed xy write the products of each pair of items from the x and y columns: thus, —6 times —4 is 24.

6. Add each of the columns x^2, y^2, and xy.

7. Using these three totals apply the formula

$$\frac{\text{sum of } xy}{\sqrt{\text{sum of } x^2 \text{ times sum of } y^2}}$$

This is $\dfrac{84}{\sqrt{132 \times 56}} = \cdot 977$

This is a very high correlation and by observing a child's score on test X, one could make a confident prediction of his placing on test Y.

PRODUCT-MOMENT CORRELATION TABLE

Scorers	Raw Scores on test X	Raw Scores on test Y	x	y	x²	y²	xy
A	1	1	—6	—4	36	16	24
B	3	2	—4	—3	16	9	12
C	4	4	—3	—1	9	1	3
D	6	4	—1	—1	1	1	1
E	8	5	1	0	1	0	0
F	7	2	2	2	4	4	4
G	11	8	4	3	16	9	12
H	14	9	7	4	49	16	28
	—	—					
	8)56	8)40			132	56	84
	—	—			—	—	—
	7 av.	5 av.					

The average or mean deviation

To find the average deviation of the set of scores 2, 3, 6, 8, 11.
1. Find the average:

$$\frac{2+3+6+8+11}{5} = 6$$

2. Find the differences between each score and the average: 6—2 = 4; 6—3 = 3; 6—6 = 0; 8—6 = 2; 11—6 = 5.

3. Average the differences:

$$\frac{4+3+0+2+5}{5} = 2 \cdot 8$$

4. The average or mean deviation is 2·8.
   The formula for finding the average or mean deviation is:

$$\frac{\text{The sum of the deviations from the mean}}{\text{number of items}} \quad \text{or} \quad \frac{\Sigma d}{N}$$

The standard deviation

To find the standard deviation of the set of numbers, 2, 3, 6, 8, 11.
1. Find the average: 6 (from above)
2. Find the difference between each score and the average: 4, 3, 0, 2, 5 (from above).
3. Square each difference: 16, 9, 0, 4, 25.

4. Average the squared differences: $\dfrac{16+9+0+4+25}{5} = 10\cdot8$

5. Find the square root of the average of the squared differences:
$\sqrt{10\cdot8} = 3\cdot29$.

Standard deviation is $3\cdot29$.

Formula for standard deviation is:

$$\sqrt{\dfrac{\text{sum of the squared deviations}}{\text{number of items}}} \quad \text{or} \quad \sqrt{\dfrac{\Sigma d^2}{N}}$$

Table for relating percentile scores to standard scores

When a test is used that gives scores only in percentiles (e.g. Ravens Matrices) it is sometimes desired to express such a score as the more familiar 'standard score' having a mean of 100 and a standard deviation of 15. Standard scores are similar to the kind of quotient scores which are derived from formulae such as $\dfrac{\text{M.A.}}{\text{C.A.}} \times 100$, the difference being that the former shows

Percentile score	Standard score	Percentile score	Standard score	Percentile Score	Standard score
1	65–67	27	91	73	109
2	68–70	30	92	75	110
3	71–72	32	93	76	111
4	73–74	34	94	79	112
5	75–76	37	95	81	113
6	77	39	96	82	114
7	78	42	97	84	115
8	79	45	98	86	116
9	80	84	99	87	117
10	81	50	100	88	118
11	82	52	101	90	119
13	83	55	102	91	120
14	84	58	103	92	121
16	85	61	104	93	122
18	86	63	105	94	123
19	87	66	106	95	124–5
21	88	68	107	96	126–7
24	89	70	108	97	128–9
25	90			98	130–2
				99	133–5

the child's standing relative to a representative group of children of exactly the same age as himself, whereas intelligence quotients or achievement quotients relate the child's score to that which is normal for children who may be older or younger than himself.

In the table on p. 152 it can be seen that the percentile scores of 25, 50 75, correspond respectively to standard scores of 90, 100, 110.

Further reading

BURT, C., *Mental and Scholastic Tests*, 4th edition, Staples Press, 1954.
First written in 1921 this has become a landmark in the literature of mental measurement.

BUROS, O. K., *Seventh Mental Measurement Yearbook*. Test Agency, N.F.E.R., 1972.
This is an expensive reference work containing detailed reviews of hundreds of classified tests.

CHAUNCEY H. AND DOBBIN, J. E., *Testing: Its place in Education Today*, Harper & Row, 1963.
Written by two U.S. test-makers this explains how modern tests are made and advises on their use in American schools.

CRONBACH, L., *Essentials of Psychological Testing*, Harper & Row, 1970.
This lengthy and comprehensive textbook is equally valuable for British and American students and teachers.

GREEN, J. A., *Teacher-Made Tests*, Harper & Row, 1963.
This practical handbook describes how to write test-items, build tests and score results.

GARDNER, D. E. M. AND CASS, J. E., *The Role of the Teacher in the Infant and Nursery School*, Pergamon, 1965.
While not primarily about tests, this contains many, some unpublished, which would interest those concerned with infant and nursery education.

MACKINTOSH, H. G., AND MORRISON, H. B., *Objective Testing*, U.L.P., 1969.

MITTLER, P. (ed.), *Psychological Assessment of Mental and Physical Handicap*, Methuen, 1970. An excellent lengthy volume by specialist contributors.

N.F.E.R., *Tests for Guidance and Assessment*, Ginn and Co.
This free catalogue, issued annually, lists and describes the N.F.E.R. open tests and gives sound advice on the use of standardised tests.

PIAGET, J., *The Child's Conception of Number*, Routledge, 1952. *The Child's Conception of Geometry*, Routledge, 1960. *The Growth of Logical Thinking*, Routledge, 1958.
These contain no tests as such, but are richly suggestive for those wishing to devise tests of concept development.

PIDGEON AND YATES, *Introduction to Educational Measurement*, Routledge, 1968.

SAVAGE, R. D., *Psychometric Assessment of the Individual Child*, Penguin, 1968.

SCHONELL, F. J., *Diagnostic and Attainment Tests*, 4th edition, Oliver and Boyd, 1960.

Largely a compendium of Schonell's tests, this book also gives simple advice on the use of tests.

TERMAN, L. M. AND MERRILL, M., *Measuring Intelligence*, Harrap, 1937.
While primarily the manual for the 2nd Revision of the Stanford-Binet Scale this volume also contains an interesting account of how a national test of intelligence was developed and standardised.

VERNON, P. E., *Intelligence and Attainment Tests*, U.L.P., 1960.
Lucidly written, this includes a brief history of testing and discussions on the principles of testing, coaching, heredity and environment, and the implications of intelligence tests.

VERNON, P. E., *Measurement of Abilities*, 2nd edition, U.L.P., 1956.
This includes a thorough explanation of the statistics relating to tests, and a critical review of examination-methods.

Addresses of test publishers

Chatto and Windus Ltd, 42, William IV Street, London, W.C.2.

Churchill Livingstone, Teviot Place, Edinburgh.

Educational Evaluation Enterprises, 5 Marsh Street, Bristol, 1.

Ginn and Company, 7, Queen Square, London, W.C.1.

Gibson and Son, 17, Fitzroy Square, Glasgow, C.2.

Godfrey Thompson Unit for Educational Research, 10–12, Buccleuch Place, Edinburgh, 8.

Harrap and Co. Ltd, 182, High Holborn, London, W.C.1.

Heinemann Educational Books, 48, Charles Street, London.

Institute of Personality and Ability Testing, 1608, Coronado Drive, Champaign, Illinois, U.S.A.

Institute for Research on Exceptional Children, University of Illinois, U.S.A.

H. K. Lewis and Co. Ltd, 136, Gower Street, London, W.C.1.

Macmillan and Co. Ltd, Little Essex Street, London, W.C.2.

Methuen and Co., 11, New Fetter Lane, London, E.C.4.

N.F.E.R. Test Division, Jennings Buildings, 2, Thames Avenue, Windsor, Berks.

Nelson and Son, 36, Park Street, London, W.1.

Oliver and Boyd, 39, Welbeck Street, London, W.1.

Psychological Corporation, 304, East 45th Street, New York, 17, New York.

Royal National Institute for the Deaf, 105, Gower Street, London, W.C.1.

Science Research Associates Ltd, Reading Road, Henley-on-Thames, Oxon.

S.E.F.A. Publications, 240, Holliday Street, Birmingham, 1.

Staples Press Ltd., Cavendish Place, London, W.1.

University of London Press Ltd, St. Paul's House, Warwick Lane, London, E.C.4.

Index of Test Titles

A.C.E.R. Mechanical Reasoning Test, 143
A.H.4 Group Test of General Intelligence, 82
A.H.5 Group Test of General Intelligence, 84
A.P.U. Occupational Interests Guide, 146
Auditory Discrimination Test, 87

Basic Mathematics Test
  A, 125
  B, 125
  C, 125
  DE, 125
  FG, 125
Bristol Achievement Tests, 135
Bristol Social Achievement Guides, 138
Burt Oral Arithmetic Test, 115
Burt Rearranged Word Reading Test, 101

Carlton Intelligence Test
  No. 1, 81
  No. 2, 81
Carlton Picture Intelligence Test, 72
Cattell Intelligence Test,
  Scale 1, 75
  Scale 2, 83
  Scale 3, 84
Cattell's Culture Fair Intelligence Test, Scale 3, 77
Cattell's Culture Free Intelligence Test, Scale 2, 75

Children's Personality Questionnaire, 147
Clerical Test FG, 132
Coloured Progressive Matrices, 64
Cotswold
  Junior Ability Tests, 132
  Junior Mental Ability Tests, 78, 80
  Measurement of Ability, English, 132
  Personality Assessment, 145
Crichton Vocabulary Scale, 66, 93

Decimal Currency Tests 126
Deeside Picture Test, 72
Delinquency Prediction Instrument, 139
Developmental Progress of Infants and Young Children, 58
Devon Interest Test, 145
Diagnostic Tests
  of Achievement in Music, 143
  in Vulgar Fractions, Decimal Fractions, Percentages, 126
Domain Phonic Test, 110
Durrell Analysis of Reading Difficulty, 111

Edinburgh Articulation Test and Edinburgh Reading Tests, 95, 108
English Language Scale, 93
English Picture Vocabulary Tests, 94
English Progress Tests, 129–31
English Test FG, 130
Essential Intelligence Test, 78
E.S.P.Q. (Cattell), 147

Farnsworth Dichotomous Test of Colour Blindness, 144
Figure Reasoning Test, 77
France-Wiseman Educational Guidance Programme, 134

G.A.P. Reading (Comprehension Test, 107
Gesell Developmental Schedules, 57
Get Reading Right, 110
Graded Arithmetic-Mathematics Test, 123
Graded Test of Reading Experience, 109
Graded Word Reading Test
    (Schonell), 102
    (Vernon), 102
Graded Word Spelling Test, 133
Griffiths Mental Development Scale, 57
Group Mathematics Test, 121
Group Reading Assessment, 106

Harris Test of Lateral Dominance, 114
Harrison Stroud Reading Readiness Profiles, 89
Holborn Reading Scale, 103
H.S.P.Q. (Cattell), 147

Illinois Test of Psycho-Linguistic Abilities, 112
Intelligence Tests for Children, 59, 61

Junior Eysenck Personality Inventory, 146

Kelvin Measurement
    of Ability in Infant Classes, 64
    of Spelling Ability, 132
Kingston Test of Intelligence, 81
Kohs Block Design Test, 70

Leicester Number Test, 121

Maddox Verbal Reasoning Test, 78
Manchester
    Scales of Social Adaptation, 137
Marianne Frostig Developmental Test of Visual Perception, 113
Marino Graded Word Reading Scale, 103

Mathematics Attainment Test
    C1, C3, 124
    B Oral, 124
    A Oral, 124
    DE 1, DE 2, 125
Measure of Musical Ability, 144
Merrill Palmer Scale of Mental Tests, 57
Metropolitan Reading Readiness Tests, 117
Mill Hill Vocabulary Scale, 93
Moray House
    Picture Test, 72
    Verbal Reasoning Test (Adult), 84

Neale Analysis of Reading Ability, 104
New Junior Maudsley Inventory, 147
Non-Readers Intelligence Test, 76
Non-Verbal Test
    BD, 75
    DH, 77
Nottingham Number Test, 122
Number Test DE, 123

Oral Verbal Intelligence Test, 77
Otis Quick-Scoring Mental Ability Test,
    Alpha, 74
    Beta, 81

Piaget Number Tests, 117–20
Picture Screening Test of Hearing, 86
Picture Test A, 72
Porteus Maze Test, 69, 76
Prawf Darlen Brawddegau, 107
Primary Mathematics Diagnostic Tests, 127
Prognostic Test of Mechanical Ability, 143
Progress Assessment Charts, 139

Ravens Progressive Matrices ABCDE, 75
Reading Comprehension Test for Personnel Selection, 109
Reading Test
    A, BD, 108
    EH, 109
Reasoning Tests for Higher Levels of Intelligence, 83

Reynell Developmental Language Scales, 92

Rothwell Miller Interest Blank, 146

Schedule D, Interests, 145

Schonell Diagnostic Arithmetic Tests, 126

Seashore Measures of Musical Talents, 144

Silent Reading Tests A and B, 108

Simple Prose Reading Test, 104

Southgate Group Reading Test, 105

Spatial Test 3, 143

S.R.A. Primary Mental Abilities Test, 64

Standard Test of Reading Skill, 103, 111

Stanford-Binet Scale of Intelligence, 66

Stycar Hearing Test, 87

Stycar Vision Test, 88

Tests for Colour Blindness (Ishirara), 144

Tests R5 and R6 (Schonell), 111

Thackray Reading Readiness Profiles, 89

Verbal and Nno-Verbal Test, 82
    Verbal Test AD, 106
    Verbal Tests
        BD, CD, C, D, 79
        EF, GE, 82

Vineland Social Maturity Scale, 137

Visual Motor Gestalt Test, 114 Test,

Visual Word Discrimination 111

Wechsler Intelligence Scale for Children, 68

Wechsler Pre-School and Primary School Intelligence Scale, 58

Williams Intelligence Test, 68

Wing Standardised Test of Musical Intelligence, 143

Word Recognition Test, 105

General Index

Age units, 31
Aptitude,
    definition of, viii
    tests of, 142
Articulation, 94
Ascertainment officers, 47
Attainment age, quotient, test, viii
Audiometer test, 87
Auditory discrimination test, 87, 90

Ballard, P., 123
Barnard, B., 109, 123, 130
Bate, S. M., 109
Battery, definition of, viii
Bayley, N., 28
Bender, L., 114
Bentley, A., 144
Binet, A., 66
Bowlby, J., 56
Boyle, E., 25
Brimer, M. A., 94, 130, 135, 136
British Intelligence Scale, 45-7
Buros, O. K., 55
Burt, C., ii, 3, 10, 11, 102, 103, 115, 153

Calvert, B., 76
Carlton, W. K., 72, 83
Carver, C., 105
Cattell, R. B., 75, 77, 83, 84
Clark, M., 114
Clarke, A. D. B., 29
Class analysis chart, 128
Closs, S. J., 146
Coaching, 17

Colour blindness, 144
Conservation of number, 117-21
Convergent thinking, 40-4
Conversion table, 13, 34
Correlation
    definition of, viii
    example of, 150
Cornwell, J., 76
Courses on testing, 50
Creativity tests, 41-3, 51
Cumulative percentages, 38

Dale Harris, 62, 63
Daniels, J. C., 77, 103, 111, 133
Darwin, C., 26
Diack, H., 103, 111, 133
Diagnostic tests,
    arithmetic, 126
    of reading, 109
Divergent thinking, 40-4
Doll, E., 139
Durrell, D., 112
Dye, G., 29

Emmett, W. G., 72
Evans, G. J., 107
Eysenck, S. B. G., 146

Fitzpatrick, J. F., 145
Flavel, J. S., 127
Fleming, C. M., 64, 79, 132, 145
France, N., 134
Freeman, G., 27
Freud, S., 56

Freyburg, P. S., 65
Furneaux, W. D., 147
Frostig, M., 113

Gates, A. I., 89
Gesell, A., 56–7
Getzells, J. W., 41
Gibson, H. B., 147
Gillam, G., 121
Goddard, H. M., 26
Goodenough, F., 62
Griffiths, R., 57
Group tests,
    definition of, viii
    value of, 9
Guilford, J., 41–4
Gunzburg, H., 139

Harris, R., 114
Harrison Stroud, 89
Hearing tests, 86
Hebb, J. O., 25
Hebron, M., 81, 107,
H.M.S.O., 10
Heim, A. H., 82, 84
Henchman, J., 131
Hendry, E., 131
Heredity, 25–7
Hesse, K. A., 121
Holzinger, A., 27
Huxley, 26

Illingworth, R. S., 56
Individual tests, value of, 9
Intelligence, quotients, 23
    scored as an average, 24
    growth of, 25–9
    related to attainment, 29
    distribution of, 32–4
Ishihara, S., 144
Item analysis, 7

Jackson, B., 26, 60
Jackson, P. W., 41
Jackson, S., 110

Kirk, S. A., 112
Kogan, N., 42
Kohs, S. C., 70
Kotik, M. L., 143

Land, V., 79, 82, 131
Language tests, 92–4
Lefthandedness, 114

Macfarlane Smith, 143
Macintosh, H. G., 8
Maddox, H., 78
Manuals, 16
Marsden, J., 26
Mayer, M., 29
McCarthy, J. J., 112
McCleod, J., 105,
Mean, definition, viii
Median, definition, viii
Mellone, M., 72
Merrill Palmer, 57
Metropolitan, 89
Moray House, 4, 6, 16
Morgan, G. A. V., 130
Morris, J., 4
Morrisby, J., 142
Morrison, R. B., 8
Music tests, 143–4

N.F.E.R., xi, 3, 4, 5, 16, 50
Neale, M. D., 99, 104
Newman, H., 27
Newsom Report, 25
Normal distribution, 33, 34
Norms, ix
Northway, M. L., 142
Number concepts, 116–20
Number readiness, 116

Objective tests, ix
O'Connor, K. P., 127
Omnibus test, ix
Open-ended tests, 41
Orally presented tests, 75
Ordination of number, 120
Otis, A., 74, 81
Over-achieving, 29, 30

Parallel tests, ix
Percentiles, 31, 35–7, 153
Performance tests, ix
Personality tests, 145–8
Piaget, J., 56, 117
Picture tests, 10, 71, 72
Pidgeon, D. A., 75, 79

Porteus, S. D., 69, 76
Postlethwaite, T. N., 79
Pre-school tests, 56–61
Projection tests, ix

Qualifications of testers, 5

Raven, J. C., 64, 75, 93
Raw scores, ix, 31, 36
Readiness tests,
    arithmetic, 115–20
    reading, 85–92,
Reading Ability (H.M.S.O.), 103
Recording results, 99
Reed, M., 86
Reliability, 14, 55

Seashore, C. E., 144
Seriation, 120
Scatter, 32
Schonell, F., 10, 78, 110, 126, 127, 145
Schools Council, xii
School medical officers, 47
Sheridan, M., 58, 87–9
Sigma scores, 37–8
Skeels, J., 29
Sleight, G., 74
Snellen, 88
Social Adaptation, 137
Sociometric tests, 140–1
Southgate, V., 105
S.R.A., 64–5, 116
Specimen tests, 3
Spooncer, F., 106
Standard deviation, 37
Standard error, ix, 38
Standard score, ix, 34–8
standardisation, 6
Stanford Binet, 30, 66–8
Stott, D. H., 139
Stuart, J., 72
Sullivan, J., 103

Tanner, J., 27
Terman Merrill, 45, 66, 67
Test Agency, 2
Tests,
    administering, 19
    construction of, 6
    cost of, 98
    culture-free, 10
    choice of, 10
    sources of, 3
    practice for, 17
Thomson, G., 6
Thurstone, J. J., 64
Tomlinson, T. P., 76
Torgenson, T. L., 143
True score, 38
Twins, 26

Under-achieving, 29–30
Unwin, D., 105
Unwin, S. M., 132

Valentine, C. W., 59, 61, 62, 83
Validity, 14
Vernon, P. E., 10, 17, 102, 123
Vision, 87, 88
Vocabulary, 92, 93, 94

Wakelam, R. B., 127
Wallach, M. A., 42
Watts, A. F., 10, 93, 103, 106, 129
Wechsler, D., 46, 48, 58, 68
Weld, L., 142
Welsh reading test, 107
Wepman, J. W., 87
Williams, J., 68
Wing, H. D., 143
Wiseman, S., 83, 108, 134, 145
Wrigley, J., 108

Yates, A., 17
Young, D., 15, 76, 107